SOME INTERESTING MEMORIES
A Paradoxical Life

by

Raymond Smullyan

Thinkers' Press, Inc.
Davenport, Iowa
2002

Some Interesting Memories

First Printing: June 2002
ISBN: 1-888710-11-X (f)

First Printing: July 2002
ISBN: 1-888710-09-8 (hc)

• • •

For a copy of our Thinkers' Press, Inc. catalog, please e-mail us (see below). Requests for permissions, foreign, and republication rights should be addressed in writing to:

Thinkers' Press, Inc.
Senior Editor: Bob Long
P.O. Box 8
Davenport IA 52805-0008 USA

blong@chessco.com

Contents

Raymond Smullyan is a unique set of personalities that includes a philosopher, logician, mathematician, musician, magician, humorist, writer, and maker of marvelous puzzles.

Martin Gardner

Part I

What follows will be more than a autobiographical account. Knowing myself as I do, I am quite sure that I will probably intersperse many jokes, anecdotes, logic puzzles, things I have read and loved, reflections about them, and other things that will come to mind as I write. I will not be at all systematic, but most likely quite "rambly," in much the way that my life itself has been. Like one lyric Chinese philosopher, of whom I am very fond, I prefer to not always remain on the main road, but to take frequent excursions into numerous side roads. And so, I will ramble along on my merry way.

I have had a remarkably diverse and interesting sequence of careers. I was born in 1919 in Far Rockaway, New York, a place that I intensely loved and still mournfully miss! My two main childhood interests were science and music. My closest friend was my neighbor, Bernard Horowitz, who went on to become an inventor with several hundred patents to his credit. I was also a grade school classmate of the famous Nobel Laureate Richard Feynmann.

As for my science interests, I built radios and also put up a long wire from my house to Bernard's house, and we used to communicate telegraph signals to each other. But my main scientific activity was in chemistry. I had my own lab in one of the attic bathrooms. Starting with a mere chemistry set, I soon added far more chemicals and glassware. I was given several chemicals by a resident chemist, which reminds me of a very puzzling thing: He told me that he had once washed his hands in 100% concentrated sulfuric acid, and since there was no moisture present, it was perfectly safe. His argument was that without moisture, there could not be any ionization. Well, that is certainly true, but is ionization really necessary for dehydration? To this day, I do not know the answer! Can some of you chemists who read this help me out? Should I believe what he told me?

As for music, my parents expected me to be a musician. My father, though a businessman, graduated from the University of Antwerp. He lived most of his early life in Belgium and also played the violin.

My parents: Isidore & Rosina, c. 1910

Here Come Some Jokes

The word "violin" calls to mind several musical jokes. (I told you I would ramble!) A man once asked a friend whether he could play the violin. The man replied, "I don't know; I've never tried!"

Another joke: A man was treated for several months by a doctor for a broken arm. At the end of the treatment, he asked the doctor, "Can I now play the violin?" The doctor replied: "I don't see why not." The man replied, "Funny, I never could before!"

Another one: A father was once proudly presenting his eight-year old piano prodigy at a party. When the kid finished playing, the father beamed and said to the company, "Well, what do you think of his execution?" One man replied, "I'm all for it!"

Another one: A cellist and pianist were rehearsing. At one point the cellist said to the pianist: "You are playing too loudly. I can't hear myself!" The pianist replied, "Lucky you!"

The following incident is true: Samuel Johnson and James Boswell were at a concert in which a violin virtuoso had just sweated through a most involved piece. Boswell turned to Johnson and said: "That piece must have been very difficult!" "Difficult?" replied Johnson, "I wish it had been impossible!"

Another true one: The pianists Rachmaninoff and Godowski once attended a concert in which the pianist at one point lost his memory. "Wasn't it terrible," Rachmaninoff said, after the concert, "The notes he forgot?" "Not as bad," replied Godowski, "as the notes he remembered!"

Another mean one: Someone once went backstage to the pianist Artur Rubinstein after a concert and asked whether he could please have three autographs. "Certainly," replied Rubinstein, "but why do you want three?" "Oh," replied the man, "I know someone with whom I can trade three Rubinsteins for one Horowitz."

Speaking of Rubinstein, I once heard him interviewed on the radio by a rather stupid reporter. At one point, the reporter asked out of the blue: "Mr. Rubinstein, do you believe in God?" There was a tense silence. Then Rubinstein sharply replied: "No!" He continued, "What I believe in is something much greater!" He then spoke of the joy in life.

I am reminded of the riddle: What is it that's greater than God, the dead eat it, and if the living eat it, they die? [This is **Puzzle #1**. Answers to all puzzles are given in Part IV].

• • •

Continuing with musical jokes, a man went backstage following a recital given by a close friend. To play a little joke on him he said, "I think you played well; I don't care what people say!"

Related to this is the following true incident: A friend of mine, an eminent musicologist, attended a concert in which his friend played a Beethoven sonata very badly. Backstage my friend said to him, "*You* couldn't have played it better!" His friend did not realize the ambiguity and felt quite flattered!

Speaking of ambiguities, the funniest I ever came across was in a novel in which I read a sentence the wrong way and was quite

7

shocked. The sentence was, "There was a picture of Queen Victoria hanging in the library." Another cute ambiguity, "My wife and I once entered a restaurant and read a sign: "Please wait for the hostess to be seated."

The following is not an ambiguity, but an illogicality. About twenty years ago, smoking was allowed on buses but only in the last two rows. Well, I smoked at the time and was once in the back row of a bus and shortly after starting, the driver's voice came over the loudspeaker, "Federal regulations strictly forbid smoking only in the last two rows." I was tempted to move up front and take a smoke!

A radical in Greenwich Village, New York, was delivering an oration on a soap box, bewailing the plight of the poor. He said, "...and an artist without paint can't paint unless he has canvases!"

I once saw in a diner a sign that read, "We cater to schools, clubs and other occasions." Another restaurant had an outdoor sign: "Specials: Mondays, roast beef. Tuesdays, closed." Another restaurant had a sign: "Good food is not cheap. Cheap food is not good." There is nothing illogical about that, but it raises an interesting question: Do the two sentences say the same thing or different things? Many people think they say different things. Well, *logically* they are wrong, though psychologically they have a point: Logically, both sentences say nothing more nor less than that no food is both good and cheap. However, psychologically, they convey different images: The sentence "Cheap food is not good" makes one think of cheap bad food, whereas "Good food is not cheap" makes one think of good expensive food.

Coming back to musical anecdotes, I like what Mark Twain said about the music of Richard Wagner, "It's probably not as bad as it sounds."

I'm also reminded of the story that Wagner was once walking down a street in Berlin and came across an organ grinder grinding out one of Wagner's overtures, Wagner stopped and said to him, "As a matter of fact, you are playing it too fast!" The organ grinder replied, "Oh, thank you Herr Wagner, thank you!" The next day Wagner returned to the same spot, and there was the organ grinder grinding out the overture at the correct tempo. There was a sign reading: PUPIL OF RICHARD WAGNER.

I also recall a contemporary play in which the whole scene took place in Hell. A visitor was surprised when told by the Devil that Richard Wagner was in Hell. "Of course," said the Devil, "he was a vicious anti-Semite!" "Oh," replied the visitor, "but he wrote such beautiful music!" "Ah," replied the Devil, "his music went to Heaven. *He* went to Hell."

I am further reminded of the joke in which a very rich but stingy man tried to get into Heaven. "What have you ever done for Humanity?" asked St. Peter. "Well, I once gave a nickel to charity." "So?" "Well, I once gave a nickel to the Salvation Army." "So?" "Well, the other day a beggar asked me for some money and I gave him a nickel." At this point, St. Peter turned to God and asked, "What should I do with this fellow?" God replied, "Give him back his fifteen cents and tell him to go to Hell!"

Speaking of Hell, I have often wondered about the following: To those of you who believe in Heaven and Hell, suppose that when you get to Heaven, God says to you and the other elect, "I know that there has been much controversy about whether Hell is really a good thing or not. Well, I have my own ideas on the subject, but I want you all to be happy, and so I shall let you vote on the matter. If more than fifty percent of you vote for the abolition of Hell, I will abolish it." Now my question is: How would you vote? I have asked this of many people and got some interesting responses. Some say, "Of course, I would want it abolished!" Others have said, "I would want Hell retained. Those sinners *deserve* it!" Another said, "I would want Hell retained, because Heaven and Hell are two sides of the same coin. You can't have one without the other." The most clever answer was from a theology student at Notre Dame University. He said: "I would vote for the abolition, but that may well be an imperfection on my part."

On one of my yet unpublished books, I considered the following scheme, which I called *collective salvation*. The scheme is this:

On the day of judgment, God takes the average of the entire human race. If the average is high enough, then we all pass; otherwise, we all fail. What do you think of that scheme? One Catholic whom I asked said: "Oh, that's a *dangerous* religion!" An Anglican whom I asked replied, to my surprise: "I wouldn't like that at all! I think my chances would be much less!" Incidently, an Anglican priest I know told me that he believed the references in the Bible to Hell were forgeries—later additions. I don't know what evidence he has for this, but it would be nice if it should later turn out that he is right.

The most humane account of Hell I have ever come across is that of the Swedenborgians. According to their doctrine, everyone who dies goes to Heaven first. No questions about their lives on earth are asked; there is no *judgment.* But the evil ones cannot *stand* the atmosphere of goodness, and so they voluntarily depart to another place. But they all so hate each other that they are constantly torturing each other. However, God sends his angels there to try to make the suffering as little as possible. Thus, the Swedenborgian model of Hell is not that of a penal institution, but more like that of an insane asylum!

Early Life and Music

Well, after that excessively long ramble, let me get back to the main road. As I told you before, my parents expected me to be a musician when I grew up. My father played the violin, and my mother played the piano. She was also a painter and an excellent Shakespearean actress.

As she told me in later years, the first sign she had of my musicality was when I was two months old. I was in a baby carriage out in the open one spring day, and birds were singing. She told me, "You listened carefully and then sang back the identical notes! The pitch was perfect!"

At the age of four, I had somehow learned the names of the notes on the piano (perhaps my older brother Emile had taught me). One day, I surprised my mother by suddenly playing the beginning of "My Country 'Tis of Thee." She smiled and said, "Let's play a little game. You turn your back to the piano and I'll strike some notes. See if you can tell what they are." And so, it was discovered that I had absolute pitch.

I indeed had an excellent sense of absolute pitch in my childhood, which unfortunately has been gradually fading as I grow older. Today, I pretty much hear each note about three half-tones higher than it really is. I understand that as one gets older, the shape of the inner ear changes and the same note hits a different nerve in later life than it does in earlier life. Not everyone suffers this way, but some do, like the famous pianist, Alicia de Larrocha (so I once read).

"Lucky" listening to me, c. 1930, at my home in Far Rockaway.

• • •

The conductor Eugene Ormandy had absolute pitch. One April Fool's Day, members of the Philadelphia Orchestra, about to rehearse, decided to play a joke on him. Before Ormandy arrived, they all tuned their instruments half a tone low. Needless to say, when Ormandy started to conduct, he was flabbergasted!

A related April Fool joke: The great violinist and teacher, Josef Gingold, about to give a violin lesson one April 1st day, whispered into the accompanist's ear, "Transpose the accompaniment a half-tone low!"

Another funny incident about absolute pitch: I am a good friend of the famous computer scientist, Marvin Minsky, who is married to Gloria, a second cousin of mine. One day in Cambridge, Massachusetts, I was seated next to him in a car he was driving. Seated in the back were two men from Bell Telephone labs. When the conversation turned to absolute pitch Marvin told them, "Ray here has absolute pitch." One of the men then asked me, "How accurate is your sense of absolute pitch?" For some strange reason, I didn't hear the question, and so he repeated it a bit louder. "I say, how accurate is your sense of absolute pitch?" Marvin turned around and said: "Oh, I forgot to tell you, he's also deaf!

• • •

Is it possible for a person who doesn't know a note of music to have absolute pitch and to be *known* to have it? The answer is *yes*. I know a police officer who didn't know a note of music, but who was, nevertheless, known to have absolute pitch. How? Well, he was the only one on his local police force who could identify different police stations by their radio signals.

Speaking of policemen, I once knew one who, when told that I was a logician, explained *his* notion of logic: "I was at a party with my wife," he told me, "and we had arrived late. There were only two pieces of chocolate cake left on the plate which the hostess offered me. One piece was larger than the other. I reasoned as follows: I like chocolate cake, my wife likes chocolate cake. She knows that I like chocolate cake. I know that she loves me and wants me to be happy. So I took the larger piece."

• • •

This reminds me of the joke about two men who went into a restaurant and ordered fish. The waiter brought a plate with two fish—one large and one small. One man offered the plate to the other and said, "Please help yourself!" The other one said, "Okay" and took the larger piece. After an angry silence, the first man said, "Look if you had offered *me* the plate, I would have taken the smaller piece!" The second man replied, "What are you complaining about; you have it, don't you?"

I am also reminded of the story of a banquet in which a plate of asparagus was passed around. When it came to one woman, she cut off all the tips, put them on her plate and passed the rest on to her neighbor. The neighbor angrily said, "Why do you keep all the tips for yourself and pass the rest on to me?" The woman replied, "Oh, the tips are the best part, didn't you know?"

• • •

The above selfishness reminds me of the following true incident: When I was sometime in my teens, my mother wanted me to do something for her that I didn't want to do. When she then accused me of selfishness, I replied, "Mother, please tell me, for *whose* sake do you want me to be unselfish?" All she could reply was: "You really should be a scientist!"

• • •

Coming back to restaurants, my favorite restaurant joke is about three men who sat down in a restaurant, and the waiter came to take their orders. The first man said, "I want a glass of tea." The second man said, "I want a glass of tea, and I want the tea to be hot!" The third man said, "I want a glass of tea, I want the tea to be hot, and I want the glass to be *clean!*" The waiter said, "Very well," and went into the kitchen and soon after returned with a tray of three glasses and said, "Now, which one of you wanted the clean glass?"

The following incident, told to me by a mathematician, is true: He and another mathematician were having dinner in a restaurant. After the meal was over, the waiter came over and asked: "Do you want your checks separate or together?" One of the mathematicians replied, "Separate." The waiter then asked the other one, "Do you want yours separate, too?"

Speaking of mathematicians, I must tell you the story of a statistician who told a friend that he never takes planes. When asked why, he replied that although the probability of there being a bomb on the plane was low, it was still too high for his comfort. A week later, the friend was amazed to find the statistician on a plane and asked him why he had changed his theory. The statistician replied: "I have not changed my theory. It's just that I subsequently computed the probability of there being two bombs simultaneously on a plane, and that probability is low enough for my comfort. So now I simply carry my own bomb!" [This, by the way, is a common freshman fallacy.]

• • •

Speaking of probability, once in a course I was teaching at Princeton, I surprised the class by telling them that if there are 24 people in a room, the probability is more than fifty percent that at least two of them have the same birthday. [That's because there are 226 pairs of people out of 24 people, each pair having a 1/365 chance of having the same birthday]. "Now," I continued, "24 is really the critical number, and since there are only 19 of you students in this room, the probability is very low that at least two of you have the same birthday." One student then raised his hand and said, "I'll bet you a quarter that at least two of us here have the same birthday." I thought for a moment and said, "Oh, of course! You evidently know the birthday of someone else in this room!" He replied, "No, I know no one's birthday here other than my own. Still, I'll bet you a quarter that at least two of us here have the same birthday!" Thinking I would teach him the error of his ways, I took the bet and started asking the students, one after another, their birthdays. After asking about half of them, I suddenly stopped and realized that I had totally forgotten that two of the kids were identical twins! Boy, did the class have a good laugh! This shows so beautifully the futility of mere theory not backed by empirical observation!

• • •

I also like the story of a man at the races who was a very methodical thinker. Since it was the fifth day of the fifth month of nineteen fifty-five, and since his fifth wife had just had her fifth baby weighing five pounds and five ounces, and since the fifth race was coming up, and the man had exactly five hundred and fifty-five dollars and fifty-five cents, he figured that the logical thing to do was to put his money on horse number five. And what happened? The horse came in fifth.

• • •

Mathematics professors are notoriously absent-minded. One of the most absent-minded that I ever met was the famous cyberneticist, Norbert Wiener. There are three delightful stories told about him. According to the first, he was once lecturing to a mathematics class, and made a certain statement, that he claimed was obvious. One of the students raised his hand and asked him why it was obvious. Why was it true? Professor Wiener thought for a moment, then left the room, walked around the hall and came back to the classroom about 20 minutes later and said, "Yes, it is obvious," and without further explanation, continued his lecture.

According to the second story, as Wiener was walking down a hall a student stopped him and asked him whether he had yet had lunch. Wiener responded by saying, "Let's see now. In which direction was I walking when you stopped me?"

The third story is the funniest of all and may well seem impossible, except for the fact that Wiener had very bad eyesight in his later years. The story goes that the Wieners were moving to another part of Cambridge. Mrs. Wiener, knowing of her husband's absent-mindedness, decided to condition him in advance. Thirty days before the moving date, she said to her husband before he left for school, "Now Norbert, thirty days from now we will move. When you get out of class, you don't take bus A, you take bus B." "Yes, dear," Wiener replied. The next day, Mrs. Wiener said, "Now Norbert, remember, in 29 days we will be moving, so when you get out of class, you don't take bus A; you take bus B." Wiener said, "Yes, dear." Well, this went on each day until the morning of the moving day on which Mrs. Wiener said, "Now *today* is the day, Norbert. When you get out of class today, you take bus B, not bus A! Norbert replied, "Yes, dear." Well, when Wiener got out of class, he, of course, took the old bus A, walked to his house and found it empty. He said to himself, "Oh, of course! This is the day we have moved!" So he went back to Harvard Square, took bus B and got off at the right stop. But then he had forgotten his new address. He wandered around for a while, and it was getting dark. He spied a little girl on the street and asked her, "Excuse me, but would you by any chance happen to know where the Wieners live?" The little girl replied, "Oh, come on, Daddy. I'll take you home."

• • •

After these further rambles, let me again get back to the main road. My childhood music studies were with Victor Huttenlocher, piano, and his brother Ronald Huttenlocher, violin. In 1930 I entered the piano competition of the New York Music Week Association and was very disappointed in winning only the second prize, which was a silver medal. Being the persistent kid I was, I entered again the next year, and this time came out on top, winning the gold medal.

My general persistence was manifest at a quite early age. When I was three, I liked to sit on my grandfather's lap and play with the smoke rings he would blow. On one occasion, I was sitting on his lap, and I wanted him to smoke, so I kept saying, "Moke! Moke!" He simply did not feel like smoking at the time, so to distract me, he told me a long, long story. I sat perfectly quiet, patiently listening to the story, and as soon as it was over, I said, "Moke!"

In my childhood days, not having anything like television around, we were far more active than most children today! I used to love to build things. In addition to radios and a telegraph system, I built a one-string violin out of a cigar box, having read instructions from Grolier's excellent *Book of Knowledge*. In many ways, I preferred that violin to my regular one! I really had much fun with it. I also built a magic lantern that worked quite well.

However, some of the things I built were complete fiascos! Together with a friend, I built a hang glider that didn't work. We also built a canoe, and the first time we took it out to sea, it toppled over, plunging us into the cold water. The trouble was that we hadn't known that one should put lead on the keel! Incidently, this event took place on a Sunday, just two days before the Tuesday I was to play in the second piano competition. I got up really early and while my parents were still asleep, I sneaked out of the house and with my friend carried the canoe down to the beach. When my parents found out about it, they thought I was crazy taking such a risk just before the competition. However, it didn't stop me from winning!

The Fair Sex

Ever since I can remember, I have been extremely fond of girls. My friend Bernard used to tease me by telling our friends that as a baby, the first word I ever uttered was "girl." In grade school, I was often sent to the principal's office. Why? For kissing girls! [I recently told this to a friend who said: "I don't think that these visits to the principal changed you very much!"]

Speaking of kissing, I must tell you of a cute illogicality: Once at a party, I was offered a drink. In my typically mischievous fashion I replied, "I really can't, because one drop of alcohol and I kiss all the pretty girls in sight!" One of the girls then said, "So if you kiss me, I'll know I'm pretty." Actually, that doesn't follow at all! I never said that I kiss *only* pretty girls in sight. I said that I kiss *all* pretty girls in sight, but that does not preclude my kissing other girls as well. If *X implies Y*, it does not necessarily follow that *Y implies X!*

In my grade school days, I loved to (and still love to) show off, particularly to girls. You see, I do not believe that showing off is necessarily bad; it all depends on the quality of what is shown. If one has something of value to show, then showing off is beneficial to all concerned, otherwise it is a complete bore. Anyway, in those days, I was an avid tree-climber. Once while climbing a tree in front of several girls, I said, "I'm the best tree-climber around here!" As I said that, I fell to the ground! [A perfect and most literal case of pride coming before a fall.]

Logic Puzzles

Even in my childhood, I was fond of logic puzzles. I recall that when I was *very* young, someone told me the following cute story: A certain man lived in the country but had to go to the city for a couple of weeks and told his butler to forward his mail. Well, after he was in the city for a few days, he phoned his butler and told him that he had received no mail. "What's wrong?" he asked, "Didn't any mail come into my mail box?" The butler replied, "Yes, there is plenty of mail in the box, but unfortunately you took the key with you, and I can't open the box!" The man replied, "Oh, don't worry. I'll mail you the key in the morning." [This is a good puzzle for very young children, to see if they can figure why the man's plan was no good.]

I recall that once when we had company, there was a very heated argument about a popular problem at the time. The remarkable thing about this problem is that most people get the wrong answer but, despite all arguments, insist that they are right. The problem: A man was looking at a portrait. Someone asked him whose portrait he was looking at. The man replied, "Brothers and sisters have I none, but this man's father is my father's son." Whose picture was the man looking at? [This is **Puzzle #2**.]

One puzzle that intrigued me in my childhood is this: What happens if an irresistible cannonball hits an immovable post? An irresistible cannonball is a cannonball that completely knocks over anything it hits, and an immovable post is a post that cannot be knocked over, or even budged by anything. So what happens if an irresistible cannonball hits an immovable post? [**Puzzle #3**.]

My introduction to logical paradoxes at the age of six happened this way: I was sick in bed with grippe or flu, or something, on April Fool's day. In the morning, my elder brother Emile (10 years my senior) came in and said, "Today is April Fool's day, and I will fool you today as you have never been fooled before!" Well, I waited all day long for him to fool me, but he didn't. When night came and just before I went to sleep, he came into my room and said: "I didn't fool you, did I?" I replied, "No."

"But you expected me to, didn't you?"

"Yes."

"Then you didn't get what you expected, did you?"

"No."

"So I fooled you, didn't I?"

Well, I lay in bed a long time wondering whether I had really been fooled. If I wasn't fooled, then I didn't get what I expected, which means that I was fooled. On the other hand, if I *was* fooled, then I did get what I expected, hence in what sense was I then fooled? So, was I fooled or wasn't I? A good paradox!

Emile (brother), me, and Gladys (sister), c. 1924.

New York

Shortly after graduating from grade school, the Depression forced my family to give up our lovely home in Far Rockaway and move to the City, where I started high school. To this day, I deeply regret not having gone to the high school in Far Rockaway where I would have been with my friends. Although I played the violin in the high school orchestra, I pretty much gave up the violin then in favor of the piano, which I studied for several years with Grace Hofheimer, a remarkable musician! During my high school years, I saw a great deal of my two double cousins,[1] Arthur and Robert Smullyan and their friends, all of whom have had a major influence in my life. They were all in college, and some were in medical school. They were really a remarkably intelligent and highly cultured bunch. Curiously enough, I had no friends of my own age at the time. All of my older friends were passionate music lovers and many of our evenings together were spent in listening to classical music records.

Every Friday after school, I went for dinner at the home of Robert and Arthur's parents—my dear Aunt Clara [my mother's sister] and my dear Uncle Albert [my father's brother]. Very often, friends would drop in after dinner. I very often went for dinner again the next day, and sometimes even on the following Sunday. My cousin Robby, 4 years my senior, taught himself to play the piano (he played the prelude of the Bach second English Suite)

[1] Double cousins in the sense that their father was my father's brother, and also, their mother was my mother's sister. Thus, two brothers married two sisters.

Far Rockaway, c. 1925. L to R: Uncle Albert, cousin Robby, Isidore (father), Gladys, Aunt Clara, me, cousin Arthur, and Rosina (mother).

and was, at the time, an art student at CCNY. He would often spend the evening painting while we were all listening to music. He later became a professional painter and art dealer under the name of *Robert Sloan.*

His knowledge of the musical literature was phenomenal. He could sing virtually any theme in the entire output of the classical composers. His brother Arthur, two years older than Robert, was at that time a philosophy student at CCNY. He went on to get his Ph.D. from Harvard and became a philosophy professor. He was about the keenest arguer I have ever known, with an excellent sense of humor.

I must tell you the following delightful incident about him: He was taking a philosophy course at CCNY with the renowned professor, Morris Cohen. Arthur was incessantly arguing in class with Cohen. Finally, Professor Cohen said, "Mr. Smullyan, please, no more argumentation! This is a *history* of philosophy course, and if you wish to ask questions, I will answer them but no more argumentation!" Arthur replied, "Very well, Professor Cohen, I would like to ask a question. How would you answer the following argument...?" Professor Cohen could not but smile!

This calls to mind the following: In one of Plato's dialogues, Socrates is faulting the sophist Protagoras for taking money from his students for teaching them wisdom. Protagoras then explains that at the end of his instruction, if the student is not satisfied with what he has learned, his money is returned in full.

Well, when I read this, the following humorous thought occurred to me: Wouldn't it be funny if a student, after his instruction is completed, told Protagoras that he is not satisfied and demands his money back? Protagoras then asks him to give a good argument why he should get his money back. The student then gives a brilliant argument, at which Protagoras says, "You see the excellent dialectical skill I have taught you!"

Here is a "dual" version: Another student comes to Protagoras and demands his money back for the same reason. Again, Protagoras asks him whether he can give him a good argument. The student thinks for a while, and finally says that he cannot, at which point Protagoras says: "O.K., here's your money back!"

There is a very interesting legal paradox known as the "Protagoras Paradox." The story goes that a very talented student wanted to study law with Protagoras, but had no money. Protagoras offered to teach him without pay providing that at the termination of his studies, the student would pay him a certain fee after having won his first case.

Well, after the termination, the student took no cases. Protagoras sued him and the student acted as his own defense attorney. He argued as follows: "This is my first case. Either I win it or lose it. My winning it means, by definition, that I don't have to pay. If I lose this case, I will not yet have won my first case, hence I will not have to pay. Thus in either case, I don't have to pay." Protagoras replied, "He has it all wrong! If he loses the case, he has to pay. This is what the case is all about! On the other hand, if he wins the case, then he will have won his first case, hence will have to pay. In either case, he has to pay."

Which one is right? The cleverest answer I ever got came from a lawyer who said that the student should win the case and not have to pay. Then Protagoras should sue him a second time, now that the student has already won his first case.

I love puzzles like this, in which it is not at all clear what the correct answer is. Here is another: Three men, *A, B,* and *C,* were in a caravan crossing the Sahara desert. One night they pitched tents. *A* hated *C* and decided to murder him by putting poison in the water of his canteen, which would be *C's* only water supply. Quite independently, *B* also decided to murder *C.* Without realizing that *C's* water was already poisoned, he drilled a tiny hole in *C's* canteen so that the water would slowly leak out. As a result, *C* died of thirst several days later. The question is, who was the murderer *A* or *B?* This is highly controversial. According to one argument, *A* couldn't have been the murderer, since *C* never drank the poisoned water; hence *B* was the murderer. According to the opposite argument, *A* was the murderer, since once the water was poisoned, *C* was already doomed, and *B's* letting out the poisoned water did *C* no harm—indeed may have prolonged *C's* life, since he probably would have died sooner had he drunk the poison. And so, who was responsible? Of course, both *A* and *B* were guilty of *attempted* murder, but who actually committed the murder?

Highschool Days Continued

Getting back to my high school days, let me tell you more about the circle of friends I met through my cousins, Arthur and Robby. Now in those days almost every house had a piano and my cousins' house was no exception. I find it most deplorable that radios and TV sets have now replaced pianos in homes! In my early days, just about every family had at least one member who could play, and I have heard many an amateur play far more beautifully than many a professional! Among our circle of friends was one very talented pianist named Irma Jurist (who, I am proud to say, liked my playing). I do not know what happened to her subsequently. Then, there was the mathematics student Saul Gorn, who became a well-known computer scientist and held an important position at the Moore School of Electrical Engineering at the University of Pennsylvania in Philadelphia.

Saul had a great sense of humor. One day we were eating in a restaurant and just as Saul finished, a waiter snatched his plate away, at which Saul said, "Good, I finished just in time!"

On another occasion, Saul suggested that several of us go to a certain place, but we didn't want to go, at which he said, "Then how do you expect to get there?"

Saul once told me his theory of asceticism: "It is well-known that the longer one postpones a pleasure, the greater the pleasure will be when one finally gets it. Therefore, if one postpones it forever, the pleasure will be infinite."

Saul wrote a delightful little book (privately published) of sentences that somehow defeat themselves. He titled the collection *Saul Gorn's Compendium of Rarely Used Cliches.* Here are some choice bits:

1. Before I begin speaking, there is something I would like to say.
2. These days, every Tom, Dick and Harry is named *John!*
3. Half the lies they tell about me are true.
4. If Beethoven were alive today, he would turn over in his grave!
5. I'm not leaving this party till I get home!
6. Just tell me what your needs are and I'll see to it that it ought to be done.

Somewhere else, Saul wrote the following about me: "Those who cannot laugh at Smullyan's jokes do not know how to take him seriously."

Another remarkable member of our group was the brilliant high school mathematics teacher, Wallace Mannheimer, who I believe, had the highest I.Q. of anyone I have ever met. Why he remained a high school teacher and not become a productive mathematician is a mystery I have never solved. He had a delightful and clever sense of humor. He used to play correspondence chess with my cousin Arthur, and once sent him a postcard with the following message: "Knowing your love of chess problems, I enclose one: Where is the move?" The whole card was filled with suggestive but meaningless symbols, such as X-Y4, but nowhere could a meaningful move be found. Finally, Arthur realized that the move was, of all places, under the stamp. [Wally had just put a tiny piece of paper over the move and then placed a stamp over it.] That was typical of Wally!

Retrograde Analysis and Other Chess Topics

Chess was a significant part of my life in those days, and I used to play frequently with Arthur and sometimes with Wally. Although I was not a particularly good player, I started composing chess problems—both direct mates and self-mates. Once when I showed one of my problems to Arthur, he said: "Now, if I were to compose a chess problem it would be of a different sort. I would make a problem in which one must deduce what has happened in the *past* history of the game." I don't know where Arthur ever got the idea, but I thought it an excellent one, and when I got home, I straightaway composed my first problem in what is known as *retrograde analysis.*

What follows in the next 13 paragraphs is for those who know the rules of chess. Those who do not, may like to skip these paragraphs.

In retrograde analysis, one is to deduce from a given position some key facts in the *past* history of the game. For example, I constructed one position in which on one square rested a penny instead of a piece, and the problem was to deduce what piece it must be. [It is not assumed that either side played *well*, only that each side played *legally*]. I was sixteen years old when I composed this problem, and I have never yet surpassed it. [It is the problem, "Mystery of the Missing Piece" published in my book, *Chess Mysteries of Sherlock Holmes*, p. 29].

I composed a few more retrograde problems those days and

was delighted when on one day, I showed one of them to Wallace Mannheimer and Arthur. The position appeared to be absolutely impossible and Wally, after looking thoroughly baffled, said to Arthur, "This guy reminds me of Edgar Allan Poe!"

• • •

I once heard the following amusing story about Frank Marshall, an ex-champion of the United States. I imagine that the story must be apocryphal, but it is extremely funny! Marshall was once in a small western town waiting for a train to take him back East. To pass the time, he went into a barber shop to get a shave and noticed a chess set by the wall.

"Anyone in town play chess?" he asked.

"Hank outside will play yuh," was the reply.

Well, when Marshall went outside, he saw Hank sitting down whittling a stick.

"Would you like to play me a game of chess?" Marshall asked.

"I'll tell you what, mistuh," replied Hank. "I'll play yuh all right, but I'm gonna win!"

"All right," laughed Marshall, and they went into the shop and started playing. Well, Hank played so erratically and crazily that Marshall was totally bewildered and actually lost the game! He then said, "You may not know it, but you just beat the chess champion of the United States! Only one thing puzzles me. I noticed that you never moved your Knights. Why?"

Frank Marshall
American Chess Champion

Hank replied: "To tell you the truth, mistuh, I never could figure out how them jiggers move!"

Wally was an excellent chess player and easily played blindfold chess. He once tricked me by suggesting that he and I play a variant of chess, which is like ordinary chess, except that the Knights move Double. I agreed, and he [being White], proceeded to move his Queen's Knight to N5 and said "Checkmate." Yes, in this variant, White has an opening mate in 1.

[For example, a ♘ on **e4** could move to any of the squares h7, g8, e8, d7, d5, e4, g4, and h5 via f6.]

I have in turn, used this trick on many others, but embellish it by saying to the person, "Let us play for money the following variant of chess. It is like ordinary chess, except that the Knights move double. Now, assuming that you and I are equally good players, I clearly have an advantage, since I have played this game before, and you haven't. Therefore, I should give you odds of some pawns or piece. What odds from me would you require to play for even money? I doubt that a pawn would suffice, would it? Would a Bishop suffice? Obviously, you would play me if I gave you a Queen, but that would hardly be fair to me! And so what odds would you want?" After much negotiation, we usually settle on a Rook. And then, I mate in one. [Needless to say, I don't actually collect the bet. It's just a joke!]

Speaking of variants of chess, I believe it was I who originally invented *monochromatic* chess, in which a piece may never move from a square of one color to a square of the other color (and similar restrictions on checking the King). I have long suspected that in this game, White may have a certain win, although I have not been able to prove it.

Another variant of chess called "Chess Prime" was thought of by the mathematician Irving Kaplansky, and is like ordinary chess, except that at any stage, either side is allowed to decline to make a move. As Kaplansky told me, "There is only one theorem I know about *Chess Prime,* and that is that Black has no certain win." Kaplansky was right! What is the proof? The proof is both simple and cute. [This is **Puzzle #4.**]

More on Logic Puzzles

During my high school days, I also started making logic puzzles. My first one used a quite novel idea that I will now present in a more pure form: Two brothers, Arthur and Bernard, were having lunch together on one January afternoon. One of the brothers was born in 1932 and the other, a year later. Ninety days after the January lunch, they met again in May to celebrate Bernard's 47th birthday. Who was older, Arthur or Bernard? [This is **Puzzle #5**].

Another puzzle I made up about that time happened this way: One evening Wally gave me the well-known problem about the king who wanted to appoint a grand vizier. Three applicants appeared, and the king wanted to find out who was the most intelligent. While the three were blindfolded, the king pasted a stamp on each of their foreheads and told them that each stamp was either red or green. Actually, each stamp was red. The three blindfolds were then removed and each one could then see what color stamp each of the other two had. The king then said: "Any of you who sees at least one red stamp, please raise your hand." Of course, all three raised their hands. The king then said: "Any one of you who knows the color of his stamp, please lower your hand." After a while, the brightest of the three lowered his hand. The problem now is to figure out how he knew that his stamp was red. [This is **Puzzle #6**].

I am happy to say that I solved the problem, and a few days later, while at home, I came up with the following more complex variant: Three men *A, B,* and *C* were perfect logicians, in the sense that they could instantly deduce all the consequences of a given set of premises. It was common knowledge among the three that all three were perfect logicians. Four red stamps and four green stamps were shown to them and while they were blindfolded, each of the three had two stamps pasted on his forehead. The remaining two stamps were put away in a drawer. Actually, each logician had one red and one green stamp. When the blindfolds were removed, *A* was asked if he knew the colors of his stamps, and he said *no*. Then *B* was asked if he knew what he had, and he said *no*. Then *C* was asked, and he said *no*. Then *A* was asked, "Do you now know what you have?" and he said *no*. Then *B* was asked if he now knew what he had and he said *yes*. The problem now is how *B* then knew what he had!

The above is a difficult puzzle, and I suggest that the reader first try the following simpler problem: Suppose that instead of each of the three being given a red and a green, *A* had been given two greens and *B*, two reds, and *C*, one green and one red. *A* was asked if he knew what he had and said *no*. Then *B* was asked if he knew what he had and said *no*. Then *C* was asked if he knew what he had and he said *yes*. How did he know? [**Puzzle #7.**]

During that same time period, I thought of the following story, concerning a young man who was both extremely sensitive and intelligent. One day, he worked out a logical proof showing that the most rational thing he could do was commit suicide. The proof was long and involved, but the conclusion was quite definite. He *should* commit suicide. And so he thought of what would be the most pleasant way of doing so. At first he thought that the most pleasant way would be an overdose of opium, but then he thought, "Just because opium is pleasant in non-lethal doses, it doesn't follow that a lethal dose of opium is pleasant. For all we know, a lethal dose might be quite painful!" And so, he hit on the following ingenious plan: He would take a non-lethal dose of opium, enough to put him to sleep for several hours. He had a gun timed to shoot him in his sleep after 2 hours. He set the time machine and took the drug. After falling asleep, he realized to his horror that he didn't have any pleasant dreams as he had expected, but was simply cut off from the outer world and that his mind worked with perfect clarity, as if he were lying in a quiet room with his eyes closed. What horrified him was the thought of the boring next two hours he had to spend. [Of course, there was no way he could wake himself up.] He then ruminated over the whole situation, congratulated himself on his "rationality" and to give himself something to do, he reviewed his proof that he should commit suicide. To his horror, he discovered a mistake!

Mathematics

In high school, I fell totally in love with mathematics when I took geometry. My teachers in both semesters were excellent, and we used a simple text which followed Euclid quite closely. This was my first experience with full-blown deductive reasoning, and I was most impressed! Today's textbooks are horrors by comparison! I believe the main cause of today's educational crisis in mathematics is not the teachers, but the textbooks. If I had gone to virtually any of today's high schools, I would never have gone into mathematics, but would have hated it! Today, mathematics textbooks are about five times the size of the books in my day, about twenty times as expensive, and are enough to turn anyone away from this gorgeous subject. They mix up algebra and geometry in one single book, and the entire deductive structure of geometry is completely lost. But the books make lots of money, and I'm afraid that the textbook lobby is about as powerful as the gun lobby!

Anyway, after studying geometry, I was undecided as to whether I should make mathematics or music my primary career. Apart from my courses in geometry, physics and chemistry, I was quite dissatisfied with my high school studies. I soon dropped out and studied mathematics on my own—analytic geometry, calculus and modern higher algebra—particularly group theory and Galois theory, since I was extremely curious to know why equations of

The Biblical leader Abraham painted by Rosina Smullyan.

degree five or higher could not be solved by radicals. [I understand from my friend Bernard Horowitz, who went to high school with Richard Feynmann, that Feynmann also studied higher mathematics on his own at the time.] I never did get a high school diploma, but got into college by taking the college board exams.

At about this time, my cousin Arthur got me interested in mathematical logic, and I sat in on a course Arthur was taking at Columbia University given by Ernest Nagel. I made an interesting discovery at the time, which I thought was original, but later discovered was published earlier. [For those familiar with the subject, I independently discovered Boolean rings.]

I spent one of my high school years at the Cambridge High and Latin School, and my English teacher, Miss Butler, was a highly cultured yet most narrowly conventional lady. She once paid me a high compliment, which she hardly intended! It happened this way: In those days, I was an ardent admirer of Bertrand Russell. I once gave a Russell book to my mother to read and to my delight she said, "He reminds me of you!" Well, in Miss Butler's class, we one day had to hand in an essay, and I wrote a particularly radical one. She returned the paper with the comment: "Your English is good, but your thinking is confused! Please come to my office and see me." Well, I went to her office and we spent our time discussing various authors. I asked her what she thought of Bertrand Russell. She angrily replied: "He's like you! He's confused!" Boy, I felt good!

• • •

In my Cambridge high school days, I lived with my brother Emile and his wife. Emile was then getting his doctorate in sociology at Harvard. He is also an economist. I recall an amusing incident when his wife asked him how a certain chain of restaurants could afford to sell such an excellent portion of apple pie for only 15 cents. Emile replied, "Actually, they lose half a cent on each piece, but they sell so many that they make up for it." Yes, he had a great sense of humor!

In later years, he was in the foreign service and was stationed overseas. He relates the following amusing incident: While in Vienna, he was speaking to a Russian diplomat, and mentioned the name *Freud.* The Russian wanted to know who Freud was. Emile told him. The next day, the Russian said to him, "Yesterday, I went to the library to find out more about Freud. Now I know who Freud is, but we had Pavlov!"

Truth Tables and Acting

Soon after my high school days, I went to a small college in Oregon and met Bernhard Abramowitsch, a well known pianist in the Bay area of San Francisco. Af-ter hearing me play, he offered me a scholarship, so I came down to San Francisco to study with him. I spent a year, in San Francisco and in nearby Berkeley, auditing some courses. The first half of the year I spent mainly with Abramowitsch, living in his house. He was usually up earlier in the morning, and I would awaken to the sound of him playing those gorgeous Schubert sonatas! He introduced me to Schubert, and I have since played mainly Schubert and

Barnhard Abramowitsch

Bach. The second half of the year, I spent in Berkeley, though I would stay with Bernhard back in San Francisco on most week-ends. My time in Berkeley was unusually rich and interesting. The two main courses I audited at Berkeley were modern higher algebra and one in mathematical logic. [For those familiar with the field of mathematical logic, I made another discovery—this time, a more significant one. I showed how to convert any truth-table analysis of a tautology into a formal proof of it in *Principia Mathematica*.]

I proudly showed this to the professor and was sorely disappointed when he told me that it was correct but not publishable because it probably would not be of much interest to logicians. Well, he was right in that it was not publishable, but he was right for the wrong reasons! The result certainly *is* of interest to logicians, but the trouble was that it had been published 2 years earlier by the logician, Emil Post! This was my second mathematical disappointment.

My musical life at this time was quite interesting. I gave a public performance of the Beethoven Pastoral Sonata. I met and became a close friend of Leon Kirchner, then a composition student and now a very famous composer. He has an excellent sense of humor, and the two of us acted together in a public

Leon Kirchner

performance of the comedy *Petticoat Fever*. He was the hero and I was the pompous British lord. It was great fun! To emphasize our mischievousness at the time, we, in the course of the performance, often put in our own lines, which had nothing to do with the play!

At the end of the year, I returned to New York, lived with my parents and neither held a job nor went to school, and was considered a sort of "bum." Once at a party, when someone asked what I was doing these days, I replied, "I'm waiting for the meek to inherit the earth."

Actually, despite all appearances, my life was far from empty in those days: For one thing, I continued my independent study of modern abstract algebra. Secondly, I composed a great number of chess problems, which were all published many years later in various books and newspapers. Thirdly, these were the years in which I learned much of my magic, which I used many years later as a professional magician. During those years, I also saw a lot of Leon Kirchner and his friend, the composer, Earl Kim.

At the age of 24, I decided to reform and go back to school, choosing the University of Wisconsin for two reasons: First, I wanted to study modern algebra with an algebraist there whose book I had read. Secondly, I had two friends who had graduated from Wisconsin and gave me glowing reports.

At Wisconsin, I took graduate courses in mathematics, although I was only a freshman, a fact which greatly disturbed the administration which didn't know what the hell to make of me! At the same time, I had the wonderful experience of studying piano with the eminent pianist Gunnar Johansen. He evidently thought highly of me, because he once told a colleague, "When that boy sits down to play, it is sheer beauty!" Also, near the end of my music studies with him he said, "I now have no hesitation in telling you that I expect you to become one of our important artists." Alas, that was not to be, since several years later I developed tendonitis in my right arm, which made a full concert career pretty much out of the question. I will return to this later. I had difficulty obtaining a scholarship, due to the erratic nature of my studies at the time. My grades were good, but a mere freshman specializing so early in graduate mathematics and not taking the usual freshman courses? Johansen who, when informed of my difficulties, told me, "Don't worry; if you don't get a scholarship, I'll pay for your tuition myself." Fortunately, this proved unnecessary, since my scholarship finally did come through, but to this day, I cannot get over Johansen's remarkable kindness!

The high point of my musical life at Wisconsin was that being chosen to play the Beethoven First Piano Concerto with the university orchestra conducted by Carl Bricken and which got a really rave review. Shortly after, I accompanied a violinist in a radio performance, and soon after *that* I had my first musical job as an accompanist to the cellist, Ernest Friedlander, then of the Pro-Art Quartet. About the same time I had the good fortune of meeting and playing for the eminent musician, Madame Nadia Boulanger, who after hearing me play a Scarlatti sonata exclaimed: "Oh, you are a natural-born musician!"

Now, I must tell you something very ironic: The only courses I ever failed in high school and college were all in music! In high school, I took the required music appreciation course and at one point, the teacher asked whether any of us could accompany a student who was about to sing. I raised my hand and said: "I can. At least, I think I can."

I then did so and the teacher then said, "He is a genius! Won't you play us a solo?" I did so, and the teacher subsequently invited me several times to her house, where we played 4 hands. Then at the end of the semester, she gave me an F for reasons I cannot understand to this day! Also, after playing the violin for a semester in the high school orchestra, the professor who conducted the orchestra also gave me an F! When I asked him, "Didn't you like my playing?" he surprised me by saying, "Oh no; you play very well!" So why did he fail me? I still don't know!

Then at Wisconsin, after my highly successful piano performance with the orchestra, the conductor who had raved to many about my playing, gave me a grade of F at the end of the semester. What was the matter with me?

Here is a related and kind of amusing incident: In the mathematics department I took a course in differential equations with a very eminent mathematician. After I took the final exam, he came to me the following day and said, "Smullyan, I have not yet decided whether I should give you an A or a B. Please come to my office tomorrow where I will ask you some questions in calculus." Well, I was a bit nervous, since I had never had a formal course in calculus. All I knew of the subject was what I had learned on my

own. The next day, to my surprise, I answered all his questions correctly. To my further
surprise, he said: "Since you answered all my questions correctly, I give you a B." Completely puzzled, I asked him
why. He then explained: "Because you knew more math-
ematics before you took my
course than I thought you did.

Emile, Mom, Gladys and me.

If you had known less, I would have given you an A. You see, I am
from Poland where the sentence imposed for a crime is directly
proportional to the education of the criminal. For example, if a
doctor and a laborer both commit the same crime, the doctor will
get a much stiffer sentence, since he should have known better.
Later, I thought: "How ironic! If I had known how his mind works,
I could have answered some of his questions incorrectly, and would
have gotten an A instead of a B!" [Several years later, I met the
mathematician again and reminded him of the incident. He said,
"I must have been crazy!"]

Logical Positivism

After three semesters at Wisconsin, I transferred to the University of Chicago where, in addition to my courses in mathematics, I took several courses in philosophy with the eminent logician
and logical positivist, Rudolph Carnap.

A word about logical positivism: This doctrine regards as *meaningless* any statement that is incapable of verification or refutation. For example, consider the question of when you and I see
the same red light. Do we have the same color sensation? The
logical positivist would call that question meaningless, since there
is absolutely no way of verifying whether our sensations are the
same or different. Almost all of metaphysics goes out of the window according to logical positivism.

As another example, consider what Leibnitz considered *the* fundamental philosophical question: Why is there something instead of nothing? Logical positivism would rule out that question as meaningless. Do you? I sure as hell don't! I have always regarded logical positivism as ridiculous! Sure, they give a precise definition of "meaningful" that renders most metaphysical questions meaningless *according to their definition.* The trouble is that their definition of *meaning* simply does not correspond to what is commonly meant by the word.

Once, in a humorous mood, I defined a logical positivist as one who rejects as meaningless anything that he cannot understand. I must now tell you of a very amusing incident: A few miles from where I live in Elka Park, New York, there is an inn where the walls of the dining room are filled with philosophical books. When I asked the owner how come she had all those philosophy books, she replied that her ex-husband was a philosopher and had left her his library. "He was a logical positivist," she continued, "and it was logical positivism that broke up our marriage!" In amazement, I asked how that could be. "Because," she replied, "whatever I said, he told me was meaningless!"

Symbolic Logic and Theses

My aversion to logical positivism did not at all affect my relation to Carnap, since I only took his technical courses in things like mathematical logic, syntax, and semantics, in addition to a seminar on syntax and semantics. I learned a great deal from him. He helped my mathematical career enormously as you will see.

In two of the courses I took from him, I was delinquent in not turning in term papers, so he rightfully gave me an *incomplete* in both courses. Some time later, I wrote up both papers. When I visited him in Princeton at the Institute of Advanced Studies, I told him that I had written two excellent term papers, which I would soon send him. Going home, I felt a little guilty about having used the word "excellent" to describe my own work! But a few days later, I was reassured when I got both papers with the grades of A in both, and with the comment: "Excellent! Your self-evaluation was correct. To me, those papers were A+, but to the Registrar, no such subtle distinctions are possible. And so, I have written to the Registrar to change your Incompletes to A's." He also added on one of the papers: "I think you should seriously consider writing this up for publication in the *Journal of Symbolic Logic.*" I did so and several years later this became my first published paper, and it constituted the beginning of my Ph.D thesis. Several years later, when he was away, I wrote him asking whether he would give me a recommendation, and he wrote back: "Of course I will. You know that I think highly of your abilities and will help you where I can."

On Carnap's 60th birthday, my friend Stanley Tennenbaum (who was also attending Carnap's course) and I arranged a birthday party for him at Stanley's house. I played the piano for him, upon which he said: "If I could play like that, I wouldn't do philosophy at all; I would be playing twelve hours a day!"

Later, we all went to Carnap's house and I did several magic tricks for him and his wife. After one of them, he said, "Oh, no! That's impossible! I didn't think that this could happen in *any* possible world, let alone *this* one!"

Modesty

Good God, aren't you readers shocked at this point by my lack of modesty relating all these good things about myself? I am reminded of a story of Frank Lloyd Wright who was testifying in court about some matter or other. The judge asked him, "You are an architect, are you not?"

Wright replied: "It is not correct to say I am an architect. I am the world's greatest architect!"

After leaving court, a friend who had been there and who was taken aback by Wright's apparent lack of modesty, asked him why he had claimed to be the world's greatest architect. Wright replied, "I had to! I swore to tell the truth."

I am also reminded of Mark Twain's remark: "I was born modest, but it didn't last long." On another occasion, Mark Twain was at a banquet and feeling very tired. When he got up to speak, he rose quite slowly and said: "Homer is dead, Shakespeare is dead, and I am none too well."

No, like Mark Twain, I make no claim to modesty! Indeed, I don't respect modesty. I respect neither conceit, nor modesty; I respect objectivity. I try to be objective about myself, but my account is admittedly one-sided in that I tell you all the good things about myself, but none of the bad things, because I am far too ashamed of the bad things to make them public! And so, dear reader, whether you approve of this or not, I will continue to tell you good things about myself, but none of the bad things. So be it!

Returning to the subject of modesty, I once wrote the following little dialogue:

A. For a person of your talents, you are remarkably modest!

B. I am not modest.

A. Ah, I've caught you! By disclaiming your modesty, you are trying to create the impression that you are so modest that you won't take credit for anything—not even modesty! But I see through you! You are *affecting* the air of modesty, but in doing so, you are being most immodest!

B. It's like I said—I'm not modest.

• • •

I also like the more subtle joke about a man known as the world's most modest man. In fact, he always signed his letters: *He who is modest.* Well, a student of religion once said to his teacher: "How can he be modest when the very way he signs his letters belies the fact?" The teacher replied: "You don't understand! He is modest. It's just that ever since modesty entered his soul, he no longer regards it as a virtue!"

Coming back to Mark Twain, one of my favorite anecdotes about him relates to the time he was lecturing in a small town in Vermont and was unable to get a single reaction from his audience. He made his jokes funnier and funnier, but the audience was completely dead-pan; didn't crack a smile. He was wondering whether he was losing his touch, but during intermission he heard an elderly couple discussing his act and heard the man say: "Weren't he funny? Weren't he funny? You know, at times I could hardly keep from laughing!"

Incidentally, a typical feature of jokes about Vermonters is that when you ask one of them a question, the answer given is accurate but insufficient—he doesn't tell you enough. For example, there is the story of a farmer who visited his neighbor farmer and asked: "Lem, what did you give your horse that time he had colic?" Lem replied, "Bran and molasses." A week later, the farmer returned to Lem and said, "I gave my horse bran and molasses, and it died!" Lem replied: "So did mine."

Another of my favorite Vermont jokes is about a man who was driving in Vermont and came to a fork in the road. The sign on the left read: TO WHITE RIVER JUNCTION, and the sign on the right also read: TO WHITE RIVER JUNCTION. Puzzled, the driver spied a Vermonter standing at the intersection, so he got out and asked him, "Does it make any difference *which* road I take?" The Vermonter replied: "Not to me it doesn't."

Actually, many Vermonters themselves have an intelligent, but wry sense of humor. For example, there is the well-known incident of Calvin Coolidge coming home from church and being asked what the preacher spoke about. "Sin," was the reply. "And what did he have to say about it?" he was asked. Coolidge replied: "He was agin it." On another occasion, Coolidge was at a banquet and being "Silent Cal," he didn't say a word to either neighbor for half an hour. Finally, the woman sitting next to him said, "Mr. President, I have a bet that I can get more than two words out of you!" Coolidge replied: "You lose!" Now, that was pretty darn clever, don't you think?

Also, there is the following true incident: A student I knew at Dartmouth College was driving through Vermont and passed a farm house and saw the farmer on the porch rocking away on a rocking chair. Since he was a bit of a wise guy, the student stopped and asked him, "You been rocking away like this all your life?"

The farmer replied, "Not yet."

• • •

Coming back to my Chicago days, a fellow student named *Lester* frequently drove me around in his car (I didn't have my own) and never let me pay for the gas. Once, at a gas station, I said, "Lester, don't you realize it would make me *happy* to sometimes pay for the gas?" Lester, with his typical sense of humor, replied, "It would make *you* happy? How far can this selfishness get?"

Another funny incident that I recall from those days: One of my fellow students—call him *Peter*—was generally disliked by his fellow students. A visiting professor—call him *Professor Edwards*—was equally disliked by the students. When a group of us were together, one of them said, "I don't like Professor Edwards." Another said, "Yeah, the other day he threw an eraser at Peter!" Upon which a third student said, "Well, I don't like Professor Edwards, even though he threw an eraser at Peter!"

Kids and Lions

Now comes a particularly cute incident: A fellow student of mine in Carnap's class had two brothers, aged six and eight. I frequently entertained them with magic tricks. One day, I came to them and said, "I have a special trick in which I can turn you both into lions!"

I expected them to be terrified, but to my surprise, they both said: "O.K., turn us into lions."

I replied, "Well, uh, I shouldn't do that because there is no way I can turn you back."

"I don't care," said one. "I want you to turn us into lions."

"No, really, I can't because there is no way I can turn you back."

"I don't care," shouted one. "I want you to turn us into lions!!"

Then, the other one said: "How do you turn us into lions?"

"By saying the magic words."

"What are the magic words?"

"If I told you, I'd be saying them, and you would turn into lions."

"Aren't there any magic words that would bring us back?"

"Yes, there are," I replied, "but the trouble is that if I said the magic words, not only you two, but everyone in the world including me would turn into lions, and lions can't talk, so I couldn't say the magic words to bring us back."

The older one then said,: "Why don't you write them down?" The younger one then said, "But I can't read!"

I replied, "No, no; even if the words were written down, everyone in the world would turn into lions."

"Wondering." c. 1926.

They said, "Oh!"

Well, several days later, the older one came to me and said: "Smullyan, there's something bothering me that I want to ask you: *How did you ever learn the magic words?*" That kid really got the better of me!

Here is another occasion where I was outwitted by a kid aged 9½. It was at a university where I gave a lecture. To give the audience something to think about, I came into the lecture hall a half hour before the audience arrived and wrote in large letters the following on the blackboard:

YOU HAVE NO REASON TO BELIEVE THIS SENTENCE.

You have no reason to believe that sentence, do you? Since you have no reason to believe it, then what the sentence says is true, which gives you a good reason to believe it! Since you have a *good* reason to believe it, it must be true, which means you have no reason to believe it. So, we have a paradox.

Well, half an hour later, I entered the packed hall and slowly walked down the stairs and noticed this very bright-looking boy sitting in the front row. I could not resist pointing to the sentence and asking him, "Do you believe that sentence?"

He replied, "Yes."

I asked, "What is your reason?"

He then stunned me by replying, "I don't have any."

I asked, "Then why do you believe it?"

Mel Fitting

He replied, "Intuition."

He brilliantly escaped the paradox perfectly! Some children are really wonderful, and I have had great fun with them! My former prize student in logic, Melvin Fitting, now a distinguished logician, and his six-year-old daughter, Miriam, were once having dinner with my wife and me. At one point, Melvin didn't like the way Miriam was eating and scolded, "That's no way to eat, Miriam!" She replied, "I'm not eating Miriam."

Miriam is really a chip off the old block! That was just the sort of joke that Melvin himself would have cracked. Melvin is also a great punster. Once when someone was complaining of the cold, Melvin said, "Oh yes, as it says in the Bible, many are cold, but few are frozen." [In case some of you don't know the actual saying, it is: "Many are called, but few are chosen."]

Speaking of the Bible, how many animals did Moses take on the ark? [Puzzle #8.]

Another time, Melvin and I were driving through town, and he suddenly turned to me and asked: "What are all these signs advertising slow children?"

Another famous mathematical logician, Gerald Sacks, and his eight-year-old daughter, Natalie (now a medical doctor), were staying at our house. One evening the philosophical conversation turned to *time*. Being in a perverse mood, I took the position that time was unreal. Next morning at breakfast, the question came up about two children, and which of the two was older. "Bill is older by one year," I said. Upon which little Natalie said, "How could he be, Ray? Didn't you say that time was unreal?"

Children are really interesting! One of my wife's grandchildren, Vincent, at the age of three was about to take his first trip with his father in a plane. He asked him, "Daddy, when we go up, will we also get small?"

Vincent's brother, Barry at the age of five, once told me, "I hope I never get to be ninety-nine!" When I asked him why, he replied, "When you get that old, you could die!"

Another boy David, ten years old, once without realizing it, voiced the political philosophy of John Stuart Mill. He and his family and my wife and I were at a movie drive-in. The first movie was good, but the second one looked as if it was going to be very bad, so one of the adults suggested that we leave. David and his younger sister wanted to stay; hence an argument arose. I suggested that we take a vote, at which David said, "No, that's unfair, because the majority will win!" That was in exact accord with John Stuart Mill's precept that the function of a democracy is not only to express the will of the majority, but also to protect the rights of the minority.

John Stuart Mill was a philosopher, and speaking of philosophers, let me tell you the joke about the philosopher's dream (see sidebar next page). The psychologist and philosopher William James once had a dream in which he believed that he had discovered the fundamental secret of the universe. He woke himself up and wrote down the great secret. Next morning, he read what he had written, which was:

HOGAMOUS, HIGAMOUS, MAN IS POLYGAMOUS
HIGAMOUS, HOGAMOUS, WOMAN IS MONOGAMOUS

• • •

This is true! There is also the joke about a philosopher who

The Philosopher's Dream

In his dream Aristotle came by and the philosopher said: "Can you give me a 15-minute thumb-nail sketch of your entire philosophy?" To his surprise, Aristotle did an excellent expository job and really packed in his basic ideas. But then the philosopher had an objection to Aristotle's system that Aristotle could not answer and he embarrassingly melted away.

Then Plato came by and the two went through the same routine, and the philosopher had the same objection to Plato's system as he had to Aristotle's system and so Plato melted away. And so, all the philosophers of history, ancient, medieval and modern came down, one by one, and the dreaming philosopher had the same objection to each of their systems. Finally, after the last one had vanished, the philosopher thought: "I know I'm asleep and dreaming all this, but here I have discovered a universal refutation for all philosophical systems, and when I wake up, I will have forgotten it, and the world will miss something terribly important! If only I could wake myself up and write it down!"

Well, with iron-like effort, he woke, went to his writing desk, wrote down his universal refutation and went back to bed with a sigh of relief. The next morning, he woke up and remembered his dream and rushed over to his desk to see the universal refutation he had written, which was: **THAT'S WHAT YOU SAY!**

went into a closet for 25 years to contemplate what life *really* was. After emerging, he met an old colleague in the street who asked him: "Good heavens, where have you been all these years?"

"In a closet."

"Why?"

"To find out what life really is."

"And did you find an answer?"

"Yes."

"What answer did you find?"

"Well, it can best be expressed by saying that life is like a bridge."

"That's very interesting," replied the colleague, "but can you be a little more explicit? Can you tell me just *how* life is like a bridge?"

"Uh," replied the philosopher, "maybe you're right. Maybe life is *not* like a bridge."

Existence

The philosopher Descartes' famous saying is: "I think, therefore I am."

Well, a little boy once asked his father, "Daddy, what is philosophy?" The father replied: "Philosophy, my boy, is I *think*, therefore I *am!* The kid replied, "But where does that leave me?"

There is also the story of Descartes being in an airplane. The stewardess asked, "Monsieur Descartes, would you like a cocktail?" Descartes replied, "I think not," and disappeared.

I love the story of an ancient Greek philosopher who got interested in Buddhism and made a long journey to meet Buddha. When he met him he asked, "What is the best question that could be asked, and what is the best answer that could be given?" Buddha replied: "The best question that could be asked is the question that you have asked, and the best answer that could be given is the answer I am giving."

In the Chinese novel *Monkey*, the main character *Monkey* (who is both mischievous and lovable) goes to great lengths to get a copy of the Buddha scriptures. When he finally gets them, he discovers to his great anger that all the pages are blank! In fury he goes to Buddha and demands an explanation. Buddha smiles and says: "Actually, blank pages are the best scriptures of all! But the people of China are stupid and don't realize this, and so to keep them happy, when I give them scriptures, I put some writing on them."

Do you know the difference between a philosopher and a theologian? Well, a philosopher is one who looks in a dark room for a black cat who isn't there. A theologian is one who looks in a dark room for a black cat who isn't there and finds it!

Speaking of theology, I have often wondered why it is assumed that God favors those who believe in Him. Isn't it possible that God is a scientific God who prefers those who believe on the basis of evidence to those who believe on the mere basis of faith?

The funniest proof I have ever seen of the existence of God was given by a freshman in a philosophy course. She wrote: "God must exist, because God wouldn't be so mean as to make me believe He exists, if He really doesn't!"

Of course one could equally say, "God doesn't exist. How do I know? Because God himself told me so, and God is always right!"

Since I am a magician, I once gave Carnap the following proof of the existence of God: I took out a deck of cards, showed him a card I took from the deck, the Queen of Hearts, laid it face down on the palm of his hand and said, "You admit that *either* this card is red *or* God exists—at least *one* of these two propositions is true."

He replied, "Of course."

"Well," I said, as I turned over the card in his hand, which was *black*. "So, you see," I said, "that the first of the two propositions is false—the card is not red, hence God exists."

"Ah, yes," replied Carnap, "proof by legerdemain—same as the theologians use! Many of you are familiar with Descartes' proof of the existence of God: Certain properties are called *perfections,* and the property of existence is one of the perfections. Well, Descartes defines God as a being that has all perfections. Hence, by definition, God has the perfection of existence and so God exists.

It occurred to me that one could similarly prove the non-existence of the Devil: By *Devil* I mean a being that has all *imperfections,* and since non-existence is the opposite of existence, which is a perfection, non-existence is an imperfection. And so, the Devil who has *all* imperfections (by definition) has the imperfection of non-existence. Thus, the Devil doesn't exist.

On the other hand, the Devil *must* exist, because he just told me that he doesn't exist, and the Devil always lies!

Musical Interludes

All right, enough nonsense; let me get back to my Chicago days. We students once had the wonderful privilege of having the great pianist Artur Schnabel come to Chicago to give us three lectures. To my horror, at the first lecture, one of the students (whom I suspect was psychotic) asked Schnabel, "You don't have a college degree, do you?" When Schnabel replied that he didn't, the student continued, "Then what right do you have to come and talk to us?" Schnabel calmly replied, "I came here because I was invited. And also, I don't think you should underrate the training of a musician." [Incidentally, I once had the privilege of playing for Schnabel, who gave me some good advice.]

Schnabel was really a logical positivist at heart, in the best sense of the word, without being aware of it. At one of the lectures, someone asked him what he thought of his latest review. Schnabel replied: "I don't read my reviews, especially those of my American critics, because when they criticize, I don't know what to do about it. Now, in Europe it was different. Once after a concert in Hamburg, one critic wrote, 'Schnabel played the first movement of the Brahms sonata too fast.' Well, I thought about the matter and realized that the man was right. I then knew what to do about it—I played it slower next time. But when these American critics tell me things like, 'The trouble with Schnabel is that he doesn't put enough moonshine in his playing,' then I simply don't know what to do about it!"

Schnabel related one incident that I found most amusing. He said, "What do you think of Stravinsky, who published in the papers that music to be great must be cold and unemotional! Well, last Sunday I was having breakfast with Arnold Schoenberg and I said to him, 'Can you imagine that Stravinsky actually published in the papers his opinion that music, to be great, must be cold and unemotional?' Schoenberg got furious and said angrily, 'I said that first!'"

I must tell you an interesting incident about Schnabel. Once, my friend, Leon Kirchner, and I had just finished listening to a superb recording by Schnabel of Schubert's posthumous *A major sonata*. I jokingly said, "Maybe we should phone him up and congratulate him!" To my amazement, Leon actually called him and I listened in on the extension.

Of course we were both very nervous about taking the time of the great Schnabel, but after Leon told him how much we appreciated his interpretation, he said, "Now, this sonata is still a classic sonata and so..." and he kept us on the phone for over an hour, tracing the entire development of the sonata form!

That's the kind of person Schnabel was. The time that I played for him, he spent several hours with me. I was both delighted and amused when he said, "I am a realist. It is because I am a realist that I can sit back and be an idealist, because ideals are the reality!"

Magical Days

Back to my Chicago days. While going to school I supported myself as a magician! I did close-up magic working evenings at night clubs, entertaining at tables and working only for tips. I also entertained at private parties, and I enjoyed that life very much. I worked at several places, most notably the celebrated Pump Room in the Ambassador East Hotel and the Porterhouse Room in the Hotel Sherman. The latter room had a southwestern decor, and I first came there dressed up as an American Indian and called myself

c. 1945, New York sleight-of-hander. Photo by Herbert Kuhn, Gladys' husband.

Chief Mishugi (mishuga is the Jewish word for *crazy).* Soon after I changed to the more successful role of a Mississippi gambler and called myself *Five Ace Merrill.* [Merrill is actually my middle name]. When spectators particularly appreciated a trick of mine, I could use the gag, "And if you think *I'm* good, you should see my brother, *Six* Ace Merrill!"

I really had lots of fun, and today I sometimes long to be a magician again. In fact, when I go into a restaurant these days, I can hardly resist going to a table and entertaining the diners just for the fun of it!

There are many incidents I could tell you about my life as a magician in Chicago, but I will be content with but a few: At one table, a single man was seated smoking a pipe. He was the most blasé person I had ever met! None of my tricks got the slightest rise out of him; he just kept smoking his pipe without saying a word. I made my tricks better and better, all to no avail. Finally, when I did my most spectacular trick, he angrily took the pipe out of his mouth, slammed the table with his fist and yelled, "It's a trick!"

Many people who knew I was a magician have asked me whether I have ever sawn any ladies in half. My usual reply is: "I have sawn 80 ladies in half, and I'm learning the second half of the trick now!"

I had one rather scary experience when I asked a lady to write a wish on a piece of paper and fold it up. Of course, I then had a way of reading "secret" messages, and to my horror, her message was *May he die!* When I asked her who the "he" was, she replied that it was her husband. You see, she couldn't get a divorce and so she wanted her husband to die so she could marry her lover. God, did that give me the creeps!

One customer offered me a job working for a well-known gambler who owned a gambling house in Las Vegas. The job was to *counter-cheat;* that is, to cheat back cheaters. When told that, of course, when one works for that particular gambler, one never works for anyone else. That was enough to scare me off!

Ed Marlo

Speaking of cheating, let me tell you of the most elegant swindle I have ever heard! It is known as the *ten dollar bar swindle* and was done several times in the early twentieth century. It had to be done at a very large bar with two cash registers placed far apart from each other. The magician entertained everyone at the bar for a while and then announced that he would do the greatest trick of the evening! He first asked whether he could borrow a ten dollar bill from the cash register. The bartender agreed and got him one. The magician then had the bartender write his initials on the bill, so it could be identified. Then the magician said, "Now, you all see me putting this folded bill into this envelope. Actually, the envelope had a slit in the back and the magician got the bill out of the slit, palmed it and handed it to an accomplice. No one knew he had an accomplice. Then the magician said, "Now, I will burn the bill in this envelope!" Well, while he was making preparations for the burning, the accomplice took the ten dollar bill around to the other cash register, ordered a drink for a dollar, gave the other bartender there the ten-dollar bill and got nine dollars in change. Meanwhile, the magician had finished burning the envelope and said, "Now the bill has gone. But I will make it reappear. You will find it in the other cash register." Someone went to the other cash register and, sure enough, the initialed bill was there! Everyone said, "Bravo!"

In my magician days in Chicago, I had many magician friends, including Bert Allerton, Ed Marlo, Joe Berg, and especially Don Alan. Don was a particularly delightful fellow, with a marvelous sense of humor. In addition to private engagements, he worked at

Matt Schulien's tavern, who also was a magician. One of Don's most memorable tricks was the following: He would borrow both a pen and a handkerchief from a spectator. He would wrap up the pen in the handkerchief, have the spectator select a card from a deck, and then tell him to use the wrapped-up pen to write in the air the name of the card, and see if Don could tell from the writing what the card was. Once when I saw him do the trick, the first time the spectator wrote in the air, Don said, "I have difficulty reading your writing, because you write with a British accent. Please write it again." The spectator did so, and Don said, "I don't know; to me it looks like PEPSI COLA. Please tell me, what was your card?" The spectator replied, "The ten of hearts." Don then said, "Please unwrap the pen from the handkerchief." The spectator did so, and right in the middle of the handkerchief was written THE TEN OF HEARTS. One mathematician I once brought to the tavern to witness this trick said, "That's the best trick I ever saw in my life!

Speaking of magic tricks, the cleverest trick I know was done in the last century by the great American puzzle-master Sam Loyd, who was also a magician. He did this trick onboard a ship with his twelve-year-old son. The boy was blindfolded and his back turned to the audience. One of the spectators took out his own deck of cards, shuffled them and showed them one by one to Sam Loyd. Each time the boy correctly named the card.

Don Alan

How was it done? Loyd never talked to the boy, and radios were not yet invented; hence, electronic signals were out of the question. So, how was it done? The answer is that the boy never said a word; Sam was a ventriloquist! The funny thing is that after one performance, an elderly gentleman said to Loyd, "You really shouldn't strain the boy's mind that much; it's not good for him!"

It is amazing to what trouble a magician will sometimes go in preparation of a trick! For example, the following trick was once done: The spectator took a card from a deck. Then a basket of eggs was brought in. The spectator then selected one of the eggs, and upon breaking it found in the center of the yolk, a piece of paper with the name of his card written on it. The hardest part of the trick was getting the slip of paper into the yolk. How? Well, the magician had much earlier taken a chicken and implanted the slip of paper into it's ovary. The egg simply grew around it!

Another example: This trick was done at the beginning of the twentieth century. The magician walked into a small town where he did not know a single individual. He was allowed to go, in the afternoon, inside the theater to make his preparations for the evening show. Well, in the show, all that was visible on the stage was a table with a closed deck of cards on top and the magician sitting on a chair behind the table. A volunteer from the audience was asked to come onto the stage, pick up the deck of cards, take them out of the case, examine them to see that there were 52, all different, and then take the cards down to the audience. There he had three people each select a card and then put the cards into their pockets or purses. The 49 remaining cards were then put back in the case and the volunteer took the box back to the stage and placed it on the table. Then, without ever touching the box, the magician correctly named the three missing cards. How was it done? I have presented this incident as a twenty questions game to see if the audience could figure out how the trick was done. Usually, in the course of the game, the following facts emerge:

Question: Was the volunteer a secret accomplice of the magician?

Answer: No. The magician knew no one in town.

Question: At what point did the magician know the identity of the missing cards?

Answer: After the cards were put back in the case and on the table.

Question: With what sense did the magician know the identity of the cards?

Answer: By the sense of sight.

Question: Were the cards ordinary?

Answer: No.

Question: Were the 52 cards really all different?

Answer: Yes.

Question: Were the cards marked?

Answer: That depends on how you define "marked."

Question: Were they visibly marked?

Answer: No.

And so, the cards were not visibly marked, the case was never opened, and yet *by the sense of sight,* the magician knew the missing cards. How? One frequent suggestion was that the cards had different weights and the deck was resting on a hidden scale. Well no; the trick was done far more cleverly. Hidden from the ceiling was an X-ray machine. Each card had a spot of invisible metallic salt that was impermeable to X-rays. Each card had the spot on a different place. When all the cards were in the case, no X-rays could get through the pack. When three cards were missing, there were three "holes" through which the X-rays could pass. They hit a hidden mirror and were reflected on a hidden fluorescent screen that the magician could see.

Clever, eh? A somewhat related trick was done by Houdini: He was sent to some place in Africa to tame a tribe of savages. On the floor of his hut rested a large trunk. Neither the medicine man, nor the strongest members of the tribe could lift it, but when Houdini waved his hands over a small boy and said the magic words, the boy could lift it easily! Of course, the whole tribe was enormously impressed. How was it done?

Well, in the bottom of the trunk was a metal sheet and Houdini had a powerful electromagnet under the floor which he could control. [This somehow strikes one as a bit unethical, don't you think?]

• • •

And speaking of ethics, I like the story of the little boy who once asked his daddy, "What is ethics?" The father replied, "I'll tell you, my son. The other day, a lady I knew came into my store and handed me a twenty-dollar bill, thinking it was a ten. I also thought at the time that it was a ten and gave her change accordingly. Later, I found out that it was a twenty. Now ETHICS, my boy is: Should I tell my partner?"

• • •

Another good trick of Houdini's was this one: He, naked except for a loincloth, and a raw steak were put in a large oven with a glass door through which everybody could see. They remained in the oven for many minutes, and when they finally emerged, the steak was burned to a crisp and Houdini was unharmed. How was it done? Well, anybody can do it! The fact is that Houdini, being alive, *perspired!* If a dead body had been put in instead of Houdini, it also would have been burned to a crisp, but live beings perspire enough to save them from serious damage during the time the trick lasts. [Actually, Houdini's temperature did rise somewhat, but not seriously.]

As many of you know, Houdini could escape from a locked prison cell in a matter of minutes. Well, he was once brilliantly outwitted by a British police officer. In London, he was put into a cell and it took him hours to get out. Why? Because the officer didn't lock the door. The door was open the whole time, and Houdini's tricks which worked on locked doors wouldn't work on an open door. It took Houdini several hours to finally realize that the door was open!

Sir Arthur Conan Doyle, in the days when he was crazily involved with spiritualism, insisted that Houdini escaped from locked trunks by de-materializing and going through the key hole! Nothing Houdini could tell him could change his mind; he insisted that Houdini was lying. He even wrote Houdini a letter telling him that it was most unconscionable of him to withhold his secret of de-materialization from the world and use it only for cheap magic tricks!

Doyle was really quite stubborn in those days. Once in London, he attended a mind-reading act by a husband and wife team. After the performance, he went backstage to congratulate them on their psychic powers. The husband said, "I'm sorry to disappoint you, Sir Doyle, but we don't have psychic powers. We use signals." Doyle angrily said, "I'm sure you have psychic powers, whether you realize it or not!" and left the room.

One amusing incident: Once Doyle and his wife took Houdini to a medium to get in touch with his departed mother. The medium went into a trance and then the voice came out, speaking to Houdini. The Doyles were quite impressed, but Houdini was laughing the whole while. After leaving the medium, the Doyles asked Houdini why he was laughing. Houdini replied, "If that had been my mother, she wouldn't have known a word of English. The only language she knew was Yiddish!"

There is one incident about Houdini that I find quite touching: As many of you know, he exposed a great number of fraudulent mediums. Still, Houdini wanted to be open-minded about spiritualism and so, he told his wife that if he should die before her, and if there were any possible way of contacting her, he would surely do so within six months after his death. Well, he did die before her, and on the back of the Christmas issue of the British magic magazine, *The Sphinx,* I read the following moving message of Mrs. Houdini.

DEAR HARRY, YOU WERE RIGHT AS USUAL.
YOU DIDN'T COME BACK.

Some Interesting Memories

Paternal Grandfather

Isidore & Rosina Smullyan

Isidore Smullyan

Part II

Teaching Mathematics

Returning to my Chicago days again after this long ramble, I worked as a magician while also on the faculty of Roosevelt College, teaching piano. Thus, curiously enough, my first college teaching position, was not in mathematics, but in music.

Then, out of the blue, I received an offer from Dartmouth College to be an instructor in mathematics for a year. How could this be? The faculty at Dartmouth were almost all Ph.D's. and I didn't even have a Bachelor's degree—in fact, not even a high school diploma. So, how come I got this weird offer? It was because Carnap was a friend of the mathematics chairman and recommended me as "a brilliant mathematician from Chicago." My teaching was quite successful, and they kept me on for a second year. They would have kept me on longer, but I decided to go back to graduate school. What happened was that after my first year at Dartmouth, the University of Chicago gave me a Bachelor's degree by giving me credit for courses I had never taken, but had taught at Dartmouth. The mathematics faculty figured that since I had successfully taught these courses, surely I should know them! Actually, there was a big fight between the faculty and the administration about this. The administration thought that I should not be given a degree under these non-standard circumstances, whereas the faculty believed I should. Fortunately, the faculty won.

During those two years, I frequently drove down to Cambridge, Massachusetts and saw a great deal of Marvin and Gloria Minsky, in fact, I spent one entire summer with them. I recall one incident that reveals Marvin in a light not always recognized. We were all having dinner at the house and at one point Marvin was feeding the dog under the table. Gloria said, "Marvin, is she supposed to be fed under the table?"

Marvin replied, "No."

"Then, why are you feeding her under the table?"

"Oh, because she's such a nice little doggie!"

At the time, a good friend of Marvin was the now famous computer scientist, John McCarthy, who was also teaching at Dartmouth while I was there. On one occasion when John was about to show a magic trick to Marvin's three year old daughter, he looked quite thoughtful and asked Marvin, "Tell me, is she sufficiently familiar with the law of gravitation to be surprised by a seeming counter-example?"

On another occasion, a recently graduated mathematician came to Dartmouth to apply for a teaching position. The chairman asked him how he liked teaching. To everyone's surprise, he answered, "I've never done any, but I don't think I'd like it."

Later, at a faculty meeting, we were all wondering why the applicant had said that. McCarthy then said, "Oh, he probably dislikes lying even more than teaching."

I recall another amusing incident at Dartmouth: One night we were grading the freshman calculus exams. One of the faculty said to the chairman, "Here is one paper in which the student had the right answer but crossed it out. What should I do? "The chairman, with his typical sense of humor, replied, "Obviously, you should give him a 10 and cross it out."

While at Dartmouth, I attended an interesting course given by the philosopher Alan Ross Anderson. One day, we were discussing solipsism, the belief that no one exists except oneself. I recall that I once met a solipsist who pointed his finger at me and said, "You don't exist. I am the only one that exists."

I replied, "That's right. I am the only one that exists."

He excitedly replied, "No, no! It is not *you* who exists, it is *I* who exists!"

I said, "I agree perfectly! It is not you who exists, it is I who exists. You see we agree perfectly!"

This reminds me of Ambrose Bierce who, in his incomparable *Devil's Dictionary*, after defining the word "I," continued, "Now, the plural of 'I' is said to be 'we', but how there can be more than one of myself is not at all clear to the writer of this dictionary."

In general, Ambrose Bierce is a most remarkable author, and his *Devil's Dictionary* is particularly delightful! Here are some of his choice definitions:

Egotist: A person of low taste, more interested in himself than in me.

Defame: To lie about another. To tell the truth about the author.

Conceit: Self-respect in one whom we dislike.

Portuguese: A species of geese indigenous to Portugal.

Armor: The kind of clothing worn by one whose tailor is a blacksmith.

Belladonna: In Italian, a beautiful lady; in English a deadly poison. A striking example of the identity of the two tongues.

Theosophy: An ancient faith having all the certitude of religion and all the mystery of science.

If I were to write a devil's dictionary, I would include the following definition:

Oxymoron: This word has two meanings (1) A stupid ox; (2) A moron educated at Oxford.

One of my favorites of Bierce's definitions is:

Logic: The art of thinking and reasoning in strict accordance with the limitations and incapacities of the human misunderstanding. The basis of logic is the syllogism, consisting of a major and a minor premise and a conclusion thus:

Major Premise: Sixty men can do a piece of work sixty times as fast as one man.

Minor Premise: One man can dig a post hole in sixty seconds; therefore—
Conclusion: Sixty men can dig a post hole in one second.

Concerning solipsism, there is the amusing incident about a lady who wrote a letter to Bertrand Russell in which she said, "Why are you surprised that I am a solipsist? Isn't everybody?" Also the logician Melvin Fitting, with his typical sense of humor, once said to me, "Of course, I know that solipsism is the correct philosophy, but that's only one man's opinion."

Our discussion of solipsism in Anderson's class lasted about two hours, at the end of which I could not resist getting up and saying, "At this point, I've become an anti-solipsist. I believe that everybody exists except me!"

In one of Anderson's classes in semantics he related an incident that was particularly noteworthy. He had worked in the Navy during the second world war deciphering Japanese code. One number kept coming up that they had difficulty deciphering. After collecting much data, they realized it was an adjective applicable to persons and nations—"this person had the property, that person did not. Such and such nation had the property, such and such nation did not." They finally deciphered it as meaning *pro Japanese.* At the end of the war, the Americans captured the Japanese code book and found out that the *real* meaning of the number was *sincere.*

To me, that sounds so thoroughly Japanese! Another incident I heard about is the following: An American visiting Tokyo was looking for a bank, and saw several Japanese men standing by a building. He asked them if they knew English, which they did, so he asked them how to get to the bank. They then spoke excitedly among themselves in Japanese. Just then, an American friend of his passed by who understood Japanese and told him what they said. The fact was that the man was standing in front of the bank the whole time, and the Japanese men were trying to figure out how to tell him without embarrassing him. Again, how thoroughly

Japanese!

Here is another thoroughly Japanese story, which may or may not be true: A certain Japanese lord used to play the game of *go* with his servant. The servant was a very good player, whereas the master was quite poor at it. If ever the servant won, the master would go into a terribly frightening fury, and so the servant decided he had better let the master win each game. This went on for months, and the master's playing got worse and worse, so one day the servant decided to teach the master a lesson. The next morning he beat the master soundly. The master, in fury, took out his dagger and was about to stab the servant, who quickly opened up his robe, and revealed that he had already stabbed himself earlier, and soon perished.

Mathematical Logic

Back to my own life. I left Dartmouth, after two years, to enter graduate school in Princeton, and got my Ph.D. in mathematics three years later (1959). My specialty is mathematical logic.

• • •

While at Princeton, I heard the following delightful incidents: The first concerns a little girl in Princeton who was doing poorly in mathematics. However, during one six-week period her performance improved enormously! Her mother asked her why she was doing so much better. The girl replied, "I heard there was a professor here who teaches mathematics real good. I go to his house every day, and he really teaches real good. I forget his name—it's something like Ep-stein, or Ein-stein."

Yes, it was Einstein! The second incident also concerned him. He once told a colleague that he didn't like teaching at a co-ed college. When asked why, he replied that with all the pretty girls in the room, the boys wouldn't pay attention to mathematics and physics. The colleague replied, "Oh, come on Albert! You know perfectly well that the boys would listen to what *you* have to say!" Einstein replied, "Oh, such boys are not worth teaching!"

As many of you know, Einstein played the violin. Once, when

rehearsing with a chamber group, he was a bit out of time, and one of the group said, "What's the matter with you, Albert, can't you count?"

This calls to mind one of my favorite musical anecdotes: The composer Brahms had four friends who were chamber players. They were poor musicians, but such nice people that Brahms liked to associate with them. One day they decided to surprise him, so they spent six months assiduously learning his latest string quartet. One night at a party, one of them said to Brahms, "Johannes, come upstairs; we have a surprise for you!" Brahms followed into a room, the four took out their instruments and started to play Brahms's quartet. Well, the first movement was as much as poor Brahms could bear. He smiled politely and started to leave the room. The first violinist ran after him and said, "Johannes, how did we do? Was our tempo good?" Brahms replied, "Your tempos were all good. I think I like *yours* the best!"

Apropos of counting, the following is true: About fifty years ago, a lady I know who was a baker went into a small grocery store and bought ten pounds of butter at 73 cents a pound. She put the ten pounds on the counter and said, "This butter is 73 cents a pound and since I have ten pounds, I owe you seven dollars and thirty cents." The store clerk said, "Just a minute, lady," and wrote down 73 ten times and added them up and said, "You're right!"

The same lady once went into a well known delicatessen in New York and saw an elderly woman slip some food into her bag. When the lady told this to the proprietor, he answered, "Oh yes! She is actually an old and good customer, but she steals a little food from time to time." The lady replied, "Don't you ever speak to her about it?" The man replied, "Oh no, that would embarrass her terribly!" [There is a man after my own heart!]

I am reminded of the joke about a bartender who when receiving money from a customer would put some of it into the cash register and some into his own pocket. On one occasion a customer gave him a dollar and the bartender put the whole dollar into his pocket. At that point, the owner, who had seen this, said,

"Jake, since when are we no longer partners?"

• • •

A high school student I know was doing very poorly in mathematics. He was sent down to the principal who said to him in a thunderous voice, "Why are you doing badly in mathematics?" The boy replied, "Oh, sir, I don't like mathematics." at which the principal said, "But you've *got* to like mathematics! Suppose you don't know your mathematics and you go into a grocery store and your bill is eighty-seven cents. You give the grocer a dollar bill, and he gives you only thirteen cents change. You wouldn't even know the difference!" [Yes, this is really true].

• • •

A rather sad, yet funny, true story is about a Chinese freshman at Harvard, who had very good mathematical ability, but a poor understanding of English. He was taking a calculus course and was doing brilliantly for a while, but at one point his work dropped enormously, and this lasted for a few weeks. Then his instructor asked him what the trouble was, and the student replied, "Oh, I'm having such difficulty memorizing that log table!"

• • •

Getting back to the subject of logic, I did not publish my first paper till I was thirty-five. A friend of Marvin Minsky who had read it said to him, "Gee, that was a good paper of Ray's, wasn't it?" Marvin, with his typical sense of humor replied, "Oh, yes. At the age of 35, Raymond decided to become a child prodigy."

• • •

On another occasion, Marvin attended a mathematics meeting and passed a speaker in the hall, speaking quite fast and confusedly. When Marvin passed him, he said, "No, no your trouble is that you are confusing a thing with itself!"

• • •

My first publication pretty much coincided with my entrance to Princeton Graduate School. In my second year there, an incident occurred that was to have a major effect on my future.

The Retrogrades

At that time, I had already composed over a hundred chess problems, mainly in retrograde analysis, but had not yet published any. You see, when years earlier I first started composing retrograde problems, I did not know such a field already existed. Retrograde analysis was then hardly known in the United States, though it was known somewhat in Europe.

Since there were no American newspapers or periodicals I knew of that published retrograde problems, my problems remained unpublished at the time. Then, sometime in the forties, it occurred to me that this type of problem would be perfectly suited to incorporation into stories. And, inspired by Lewis Carroll, I conceived the notion of stories in which the pieces themselves should play the part of the main characters. Somehow, the Arabian Nights leaped to mind as the setting—Haroun Al Rashid as the white King, his grand vizier as the white King's Bishop, and so forth. At that time I wrote those Arabian Nights tales and planned to make a whole book of them one day. Well, years went by and in Princeton I showed some of my problems to several of my fellow graduate students, as well as to a logician who was then a Fellow at the nearby Institute of Advanced Studies. One of the best of these problems was titled "Where Is the White King?" and consisted of a position in which the white King could not be seen on the board because, according to the accompanying story, he had made himself invisible. The problem was to determine on which square he must stand. I showed this particular problem to my office mate and he said, "Why don't you publish it before somebody else does?" I laughed and replied, "Why would anybody do that?"

Well, a few weeks later, I met the logician from the Institute who said, "Hey Smullyan, how come someone published your problem in the *Manchester Guardian* without crediting you as the author?" [The *Manchester Guardian* is a British newspaper.] Well I saw to my amazement that my problem was submitted by the father of my office mate! I went immediately to my office mate and asked him how that had happened.

"Oh yes," he replied, "I showed your problem to my father who has had frequent correspondence with the chess editor of the *Guardian,* and he sent him your problem with the comment, "Instead of the usual type of chess problem, why don't you publish a problem like this?"

Now, the father never claimed to be the author of the problem, he just failed to state who the author was. When I expressed disappointment that my authorship had not been acknowledged, he said, "Oh, I'll speak to my father about that." A couple of weeks later, I received a very nice letter from the chess editor of the *Manchester Guardian* expressing regret that he had not known that I was the author of this "delightful work," and assuring me that my authorship would be acknowledged in the next issue. He also asked me if I had any more chess problems that I could send him, so in the next few months I published several problems in the *Manchester Guardian,* which led to the publication of others in European and Canadian journals.

Several years later, a remarkable thing happened. The same problem, "Where Is the White King?," came out in Martin Gardner's column in *Scientific American* without mention of my authorship! It had been sent in by a correspondent, with a note saying that while he found it remarkable, he did not know who had originated it. I knew nothing about this at the time, and probably never would have known had it not been seen by a mathematician, Mitch Taibelson, I knew as a student in my Chicago days. He promptly wrote to Martin that the problem had been devised about twenty years earlier by Raymond Smullyan, and that it was one of a large collection of unpublished chess problems invented by Smullyan, when they were both students at the University of Chicago. *ChessBase Magazine* recently mentioned it too.

Boy, if it had not been for that letter, my life might have turned out differently! This led to a happy renewal of my acquaintance with Martin Gardner, who urged me to stop dilly-dallying and get the book written! This goaded me to get to work.

At first, I planned to incorporate all my retrograde problems into Arabian Nights stories, but then the well-known retrograde expert and composer, Mannis Charosch, who had seen some of

my problems, kindly sent me a copy of an excellent paper he had written entitled, "Detective at the Chessboard," which was a fine introduction to retrograde analysis for the general reader. The title instantly captured my fancy and I thought, "Why not have an *actual* detective at the chessboard, and for that matter, why not my favorite one, Sherlock Holmes?"

I changed my plan and decided to divide the problems into two books, one on Sherlock Holmes and the other on the Arabian Nights. At first I decided to title the first one, "Sherlock Holmes at the Chessboard," but someone suggested to me

First of the retrogrades, American edition.

the better title, *The Chess Mysteries of Sherlock Holmes,* which I finally used. As to the second book, instead of titling it "The Chess Mysteries of the Arabian Nights," I called it, *The Chess Mysteries of the Arabian Knights.*

While working on these books, I wrote to Martin of my plan and he in turn, wrote to the chess editor of a well-known publishing company. The editor soon called me and was quite enthusiastic about the idea and invited me to send him the manuscripts, when they were finished. Several weeks later, I received a letter from the editor informing me that although he was in favor of the book, the sales department had turned it down! As he said, "Times have changed, and these days publishers want books with good commercial possibilities." So here I was, stuck with what I have always considered two excellent unpublished manuscripts!

About that time, Melvin Fitting's father-in-law, Oscar Collier, literary agent and editor for Prentice-Hall, asked Melvin if he was interested in writing a book of *logic* puzzles. Mel told him it was really not his line and that I would be a good person to do that. Hence, Oscar got in touch with me, and I told him about my chess books. He said he wasn't interested in chess problems; what he wanted were *logic* problems. And so I set to work composing my first book of logic puzzles titled *What Is the Name of This Book?*

After I had written a few chapters, I had lunch with Oscar and brought him the chapters of my chess books as well. As he told me before, he was not interested in my chess books for Prentice-Hall, but would propose my book of logic puzzles. As for the chess books, he, as a literary agent, would try to find a publisher for them.

He got my logic puzzle book published by Prentice-Hall, and he sent my chess books to Alfred A. Knopf, where they were looked at by Ann Close, a senior editor. She quickly sent them back, telling Oscar that "chess was out of her line."

Then *What Is the Name of This Book?* came out and received a rave review from Martin Gardner who pronounced it as "the best book of recreational logic puzzles ever written." When Ann read this, she telephoned Oscar and asked for a second look at my chess books. Ann is an extremely clever lady who knew virtually nothing about chess when she started her second look but applied herself so thoroughly, that after a month she had enough expertise to understand my chess problems, and even to find mistakes in some of them!

Knopf published both books, and that's the story of how my chess books got published. [Incidentally, my problem, "Where Is the White King?" is the problem that appears on the front cover of the jacket of The Arabian Knights.]

I have subsequently published many puzzle books with Alfred Knopf with Ann Close as my editor including *The Lady or the*

Tiger; To Mock a Mockingbird; Forever Undecided; Satan, Cantor and Infinity; and *The Riddle of Scheherezade.*

I also published the puzzle book *Alice in Puzzleland* with William Morrow and Company. These books are actually far more than mere puzzle books. The puzzles were designed to lead the reader into some deep results in mathematical logic such as Gödel's famous theorems, which I now wish to discuss.

Gödel and Island Truth-Tellers

In the early part of the 20th century appeared two comprehensive mathematical systems—so comprehensive, in fact, that it was taken for granted that every mathematical statement could either be proved or disproved within the system. In 1933, Kurt Gödel proved that this was not the case. In each of the systems he found a sentence which though true, could not be proved in the system! If this true system is added as another axiom to the system, another sentence emerges which is both true and not provable in the system! And Gödel showed that any system adequate for a certain large body of mathematics must suffer from the limitation that there are sentences which, though true, are not provable in the system. This was known as Gödel's *first* incompleteness theorem. Next, he showed the even more remarkable result that each such system, if consistent could not prove its own consistency! Thus, if the system could prove

its own consistency, it would become inconsistent in the process! This was known as Gödel's *second* incompleteness theorem.

Here is a very rough sketch of the central idea behind the proof of Gödel's first incompleteness theorem. In the systems subject to Gödel's proof, the objects that the sentences were about were not sentences themselves, but abstract sets and numbers. Gödel got around this by coding sentences into numbers. He assigned to each sentence of the system a unique number called the *Gödel number* of the sentence.

He then constructed a most ingenious sentence *G* that asserted that a certain number *n* was *not* the Gödel number of a sentence that was provable in the system. The ingenious thing was that *n* was the Gödel number of the very sentence *G* itself! Thus *G* asserted that its own Gödel number was not the Gödel number of a provable sentence, which is tantamount to saying that *G* asserted that it was not provable in the system. Thus *G* is true if *and only if G* is not provable in the system. This means that either *G* is true and not provable (in the system), as *G* asserts, or that *G* is false (not true) but provable in the system. The latter is ruled out by the fact that the system is obviously correct, in that it never proves any false sentence. Hence, the first alternative must hold—*G* is true but not provable in the system.

I have devised many puzzles to popularly illustrate Gödel's idea, and here is one of them: On a certain island, every native is of one of two types—*truth-tellers*, who make only true statements and *liars*, who make only false ones. **Everything a truth-teller says is true and everything a liar says is false.** One day, a certain logician visited this island. The logician was 100% accurate in his beliefs and the things he could prove; he never gave a proof of a false statement. The logician met a native who made a statement from which it follows that he must be a truth teller, but it was logically impossible for the logician to ever prove that he was! What statement would work? [You might like to try to solve this before reading further].

One solution is that the native said, "You can never prove that I am a truth-teller." If the native was not a truth-teller, his statement would be false, hence what he *said* would not be the case, which means that the logician *could* prove that the native was a truth-teller, whereas the native really was not. This is contrary to the given condition that the logician never proves false propositions. Therefore, the native must be a truth teller. It further follows that what he said must be true, which means that the logician can never prove that he is a truth teller. Thus, the native must be a truth-teller, but the logician can never prove that he is. [The native's statement: "You can never prove that I am a truthteller." corresponds to Gödel's sentence that in effect says "I am not provable."]

Another illustration: Suppose that on this island some of the truth-tellers have been designated *certified truth-tellers*. You visit this island and meet a native who makes a statement from which you can deduce that he must be a truth-teller, but not a certified one. What statement would work? Well, one possible statement that works is, "I am not a certified truth-teller." If he were a liar, his statement would be false, which would mean that he *is* a certified truth-teller, which is impossible for a liar! Therefore, he is a truth-teller. It further follows that since his statement was true, he is not a certified truth-teller, as he said, and so he must be an uncertified truth-teller.

The analogy to Gödel's construction is this: The truth-tellers correspond to the sentences of the mathematical system that are *true*. The *certified truth-tellers* correspond to the sentences that are not only true, but provable in the system. So, the native who says, "I am not a certified truth-teller." is the counterpart of Gödel's sentence which effectively says: "I am not provable."

On this same island, some of the liars are also designated as *certified liars*. What statement could a native make that would convince you that he is a certified liar? [**Puzzle #9.**]

For further variants, what statement could a native make from which it could be deduced that he must be certified (either as a truth-teller or a liar) with no way of knowing whether he is a truth-teller or a liar? [**Puzzle #10.**]

What statement could he make that would convince you that he was either a certified truth-teller or an uncertified liar, but no way of telling which? [**Puzzle #11.**]

Incidentally, it is puzzles like the last one that inspired Melvin Fitting to once introduce me as a speaker at a mathematics meeting by saying, "I now introduce Professor Smullyan who will prove to you that either he doesn't exist or you don't exist, but you won't know which!"

I must tell you of two other funny introductions I have had: In one of them, the speaker who introduced me by saying that I was unique. I couldn't resist interrupting him and saying: "I'm sorry to interrupt you sir, but I happen to be the only one in the entire universe who is *not* unique!"

The funniest introduction I ever got was from the philosopher Nuel Belnap Jr. who said, "I promised myself three things in this introduction—one, to be brief, two, not to be facetious, and three, not to refer to this introduction."

Liars and truth-tellers have played a big role in my puzzle books, though called by different names such as *knights* (truth-tellers) and *knaves* (liars), but I shall here continue with the present terminology. Here is a typical puzzle of this type: One day a prospector went to this island, because there was a rumor that gold was to be found there. He met a native and asked him, "Is there gold on this island?" The native replied: "Either I am a liar or there is gold on this island." Can it be determined whether or not he is a truth-teller? Can it be determined whether there is gold on the island? [**Puzzle #12.**]

There is another island in which again each inhabitant either always tells the truth or always lies, but there is a firmly held

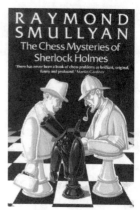

British version.

taboo there against ever using English words, despite the fact that all the natives understand English perfectly. And so, whenever a yes/no question is asked of a native, he answers in his native language—he answers either *Bal* or *Da*. One of the words means *yes* and the other means *no;* but it is not given which word means which. One day, a visitor came to the island and asked a native: "Does *Bal* mean *Yes?*" The native answered, "Bal." Can it be determined what *Bal* means? Can it be determined whether the native's answer was true or false? [**Puzzle #13.**]

Another problem: What yes/no question should one ask a native to find out what *Bal* really means? [**Puzzle #14.**]

I am assuming in these puzzles that the natives know the correct answers to questions asked and that when they make statements, they know whether they are true or not, because lying doesn't mean making false statements; it means making statements that one *believes* to be false.

An amusing illustration of this is a true case that I once read in a psychology textbook: The doctors of a certain mental institution were thinking of releasing a certain schizophrenic patient. They decided to first give him a test under a lie detector. One of the questions they asked him was: "Are you Napoleon?" He replied: "No." The machine showed he was lying!

I just thought of a riddle: A certain man went around claiming he was Napoleon. He wasn't lying; he really *believed* that he was! Yet the man was not insane. How is this to be explained? [**Puzzle #15.**]

This may be hard to believe, but in a psychology book written in 1901, I came across the word "schizophrenia" defined as a mental disease resulting from disobedience to one's parents!

I once thought of the following definition: *Schizophrenic* - one who keeps forging his own signature.

I also like the following verse:

> *Roses are red.*
> *Violets are blue.*
> *I'm a schizophrenic,*
> *And so am I.*

Here is another problem about the first island of truth-tellers and liars: A man visits this island and comes across a native who was lazily lying in the sun. The man remembers that the native's name was either *Edward* or *Edwin* but he couldn't remember which. He asked the native whether his name was Edward or Edwin, and the native said, "Edward." Was his name Edward or Edwin? [**Puzzle # 16.**]

When you have read the solution to the above problem, you will see why the problem has a resemblance to the following incident: When I was in England, I gave the following proof to a British logician (call him Bill) that in England people drive on the wrong side of the road. (As you must know, they drive on the left side).

Me: In America we drive on the right side of the road, don't we?

Bill: Yes.

Me: In England you don't drive on the right side, do you?

Bill: No.

Me: Therefore, you drive on the wrong side.

I also gave him the following irresistible argument that Santa Claus exists:

Me: Santa Claus exists, if I am not mistaken.

Bill: Of course, Santa Claus exists *if you are not mistaken.*

Me: So I was right.
Bill: Yes.
Me: So I was not mistaken.
Bill: Yes.
Me: Hence Santa Claus exists.

Here is another proof of the existence of Santa Claus. Consider the following sentence:

EITHER THIS SENTENCE IS FALSE OR SANTA CLAUS EXISTS.

The underlying logic here is the same as that of Problem #12: If the sentence were false, then it *would* be the case that *either* the sentence is false *or* Santa Claus exists—at least one of the two alternatives would hold since the first would; hence what the sentence said would be true, and we would have a contradiction. Therefore, the sentence can't be false; it must be true—one of the two alternatives must hold. But since the first doesn't (the sentence is not false, but true), it must be the second alternative that holds. Thus Santa Claus exists.

Now that I have had my fun, let me get back to telling you how I use recreational logic puzzles to illustrate significant mathematical results. Let us go back to the first island of liars and truth-tellers, in which English is spoken. A native there was heard to say, "This is not the first time I have said what I am now saying." Was he a liar or a truth-teller? [**Puzzle #17.**]

On another occasion a native said: "This is the first time I have said what I am now saying." Can it be determined whether he is a liar or a truth-teller? [**Puzzle #18.**]

I must interrupt myself at this point and tell you of a funny fantasy I once had: It was about a child who at the age of five had not yet spoken. At the age of ten, he had still not spoken. At the age of twenty, he had not yet spoken.——At the age of eighty-one he had not yet spoken, and just before he died, he turned to the company present and said: "I have nothing more to say!"

• • •

This reminds me of the following true incident a psychologist once told me. A psychotic patient who had not spoken for sixteen years was being exhibited to a medical class. One of the wise-guy students went up to him and asked: "Why don't you ever say anything?" To everybody's surprise, the patient said: "What is there to say?"

I am also reminded that right before he died, Oscar Wilde said, "I am dying beyond my means!"

Oscar Wilde was once at a party and one of the company made a clever remark, at which Oscar Wilde said, "I wish I had said that!" at which someone else then said, "Don't worry, Oscar, you will!"

It is interesting how sometimes scholars of humor have no sense of humor themselves! The philosopher Henri Bergson, who wrote a book on *Laughter*, was once at a party at which George Bernard Shaw was present and was explaining Bergson's philosophy to the group. At one point, Bergson interrupted and said: "No, no, monsieur, that is not at *all* what I meant!" Shaw replied, "Please, I understand your philosophy much better than you do!" Bergson did not at all see the humor of this and was furious!

• • •

I indicated before that the last two puzzles were related to a significant mathematical result, and you will later see that it is so, but first I wish to give you a forward version by means of a story I have written elsewhere.

The story is about a man who was in search of immortality and read all sorts of alchemy books, but could not find anything *practical* in them. Then, he heard of a great sage in the East who was a specialist in this area, and so he went on a pilgrimage to find him. After twelve years, he found the sage and asked him, "Is it really possible for one to live forever?"

The sage replied, "Oh, quite easily, providing he does two things."

"And what are those things?" the man asked eagerly.

"The first thing is to always tell the truth, never make any false statement. That's a small price to pay for immortality, isn't it?"

"Of course," replied the man, "and what is the second thing?"

The second thing," replied the sage, "is to say 'I will repeat this sentence tomorrow.' If you do those two things, I guarantee that you will live forever!"

The man thought for a moment and said: "Oh, of course, if I do those two things I will live forever, because if I truthfully say that sentence today, then I will indeed repeat it tomorrow, and when I truthfully say it again tomorrow, I will truthfully repeat it again the next day, and so forth. But your solution is not a *practical* one! How can I be sure of *truthfully* saying that I will repeat this sentence tomorrow if I can't be sure of being alive tomorrow! Your solution is not a practical one!"

"Oh," replied the sage, "you wanted a *practical* solution! No, I don't deal with practice; I deal only with theory."

• • •

Now, the above story, as well as the last two problems illustrate the principle known as *mathematical induction*. Before stating this in its generality, I believe it will make it easier to grasp if I first give you an example.

Suppose you are told that on a certain planet it is raining today, and it never happens that it rains on any day there without raining also on the next day as well, that is, on any day in which it rains, it also rains the next day. Isn't it obvious that under those conditions it will rain on all days evermore on this planet? Well, this is but a special case of the principle of *mathematical induction,* which is that if a certain property holds for the number 1, and never holds for any number (positive whole number) without also holding for the next number, then the property must hold for *all* positive whole numbers 1, 2, 3,... . That's all that mathematical induction really is! When made precise, the proof that in the story of the search for immortality, the sage's two conditions really do imply immortality—this proof is really by mathematical induction. Indeed, often the phrase "and so forth" is the informal counterpart of mathematical induction.

I also like to illustrate mathematical induction in the following manner: Imagine that we are all immortal and let us go back to the days when the milkman would leave milk at our back doors. The housewife would leave a note telling the milkman what to do. Now, suppose the housewife leaves the following note:

NEVER LEAVE MILK ON ANY DAY
WITHOUT LEAVING MILK THE
NEXT DAY AS WELL.

Well, the milkman could go on thousands of years without ever leaving milk at all without disobeying the housewife's instructions. If she should then complain and ask the milkman why he disobeyed her order, he could rightfully say: "I didn't disobey your order! Did I ever leave milk one day without leaving milk the next day? No, I never left milk at all!" Well, suppose the milkman goes another thousand years without leaving milk, then on a whim one day, he leaves milk. He is then committed to leave milk on all days forever more! We now see that the above note of the housewife is quite inadequate. Now, the following note *is* adequate:

1. ON ANY DAY THAT YOU LEAVE MILK,
LEAVE MILK THE NEXT DAY AS WELL.
2. LEAVE MILK TODAY.

Those two instructions will do the job—they guarantee permanent delivery.

The computer scientist, Alan Tritter had the following cute idea which involves a note with only one instruction:

*LEAVE MILK TODAY AND READ
THIS NOTE AGAIN TOMORROW.*

Valid vs. Sound Arguments

I would like now to say a little more about logic in general. There is a difference between the notions of a *valid* argument and a *sound* argument.

A *valid* argument is one in which the conclusion logically follows from the premises, regardless of whether the premises themselves are true or not.

A *sound* argument is an argument that is not only valid, but also such that the premises of the argument are actually true.

The conclusion of a sound argument must, of course, be true, but the conclusion of a valid argument may well be false. As examples, the following argument is not only valid, but sound:

*ALL MEN ARE MORTAL.
SOCRATES IS A MAN.
THEREFORE, SOCRATES IS MORTAL.*

The following argument, though clearly not sound *is* valid.

*ALL BATS CAN FLY.
SOCRATES IS A BAT.
THEREFORE SOCRATES CAN FLY.*

The second premise is obviously false. If it were true, if Socrates were a bat, then he could fly.

Now consider the following argument:

*EVERYONE LOVES MY BABY.
MY BABY LOVES ONLY ME.
THEREFORE I AM MY OWN BABY.*

Is that argument valid? [Puzzle #19.]

How about the following argument?

> *EVERYONE LOVES A LOVER.*
> *ROMEO LOVES JULIET.*
> *THEREFORE IAGO LOVES OTHELLO.*

In that argument, by a *lover* is meant anybody who loves at least one person. Is that argument valid? **[Puzzle #20.]**

In a lighter vein, someone once gave me the following syllogism:

> *SOME CARS RATTLE.*
> *MY CAR IS SOME CAR.*
> *SO NO WONDER MY CAR RATTLES!*

I like Tweedledee's characterization of logic in Lewis Carroll's *Through the Looking Glass:*

> *If it was so, it might be;*
> *and if it were so it would be,*
> *but as it isn't, it ain't. That's logic.*

I also like Thurber's Characterization of logic in "The Thirteen Clocks":

> *Since it is possible to touch a clock without stopping it,*
> *it is therefore possible to start a clock without touching it.*
> *That's logic as I see and understand it.*

The writer Miguel Unamuno has frequently lambasted rationality and reasoning. In reading that, I could not resist composing the following verse:

Some Interesting Memories

Unamuno gives reasons why reasons are bad,
And the reasons he gives are incredibly bad!

As we are on the subject of logic, here is a particularly appropriate joke: A freshman college student asked his grade advisor what he should study. "Logic," was the answer.

"What is logic?"

"Logic enables one to deduce certain facts from others. For example, do you have a lawn mower?"

"Yes."

"From which I conclude that you have a lawn."

"Yes, I have a lawn."

"From which, I take it, you have a house."

"Yes, I have a house."

"Then you are married."

"Yes, I have a wife."

"And children?"

"Yes, I have children."

"From which I conclude that you are a heterosexual male."

"I am indeed a heterosexual male. Gee, this logic is amazing! From the fact that I have a lawn mower, you could deduce that I am a heterosexual male. Remarkable!"

As would happen, later the student met in the hall another student whom he knew and told him that he should study logic.

"What is that?" the friend asked.

"It enables you to deduce one proposition from another. For example, do you have a lawn mower?"

The friend replied, "No." The student then said, "You faggot!"

I would like now to give you another problem about the island of liars and truth-tellers: A logician once visited this island and came across a native whom he had never seen before. The native made a statement which caused the logician to say: "You know, if you hadn't said that, I could have believed it! Before you said it, I had no way of knowing whether it was true or false, but the very fact that you said it proves that it is false! What statement could that have been? [**Puzzle #21.**]

I must now tell you two quite revealing incidents: Fairly soon after my first puzzle book came out, I received a letter from an unknown female who suggested an alternative solution to one of my problems that I found far more elegant than the one I had given. My solution was correct, but hers was much prettier. To my surprise, she ended the note with "Love" followed by her signature. I had no idea how old she was, or whether she was married or single. I wrote her, expressing my admiration for her elegant solution and asked her if I could have her permission to use it in a future edition. Shortly after, I received a letter that read: "Dear Professor Smullyan. Thank you for your gracious letter. You have my permission to use my solution. I am nine years old and in fifth grade."

So, that explains it! Some children are really marvelous! My second incident is also primarily about a child, aged ten.

When I was a graduate student, a fellow classmate was the brilliant future mathematician, Barry Mazur. Well, almost 20 years after I last saw Barry, which was shortly after my first puzzle book came out, I got a letter from Barry's ten year old son suggesting a really marvelous puzzle, which gave me an idea for a whole chapter of puzzles! I got Barry's Cambridge phone number and called him because I wanted to congratulate the boy. Before Barry put his son on the phone, he told me in soft conspirational tones, "Listen, he's reading your book and loves it, but don't let him know it's math, because he hates math!"

I once gave a little girl the following problem: Fifty-six biscuits are to be fed to ten animals, dogs and cats. Each dog gets six biscuits and each cat gets five. How many animals are dogs? This, of course, is a standard algebra problem which would be solved by letting x be the number of dogs hence $10-x$ is the number of cats, and solving the equation $x + 5 (10-x) = 56$. However, this girl didn't know any algebra, but came up with the following ingenious solution: She said, "First feed each of the ten animals five biscuits each. This uses up fifty biscuits. Now, the cats have had their portion, and each dog is to get one more, and since there are six biscuits left, there must be six dogs."

Now, that's what I call clever thinking, typical of the kind of thinking that creative mathematicians use.

Earlier I used the word "elegant" to describe the solution a girl gave me. Several people have expressed puzzlement of how "elegant" can be applied to mathematics, which is often mistakenly regarded as a routine, and mechanical subject. Nothing could be further from the truth! Let me give you a very simple but quite elegant example: Suppose you have an eight by eight board with 64 squares, like a checkerboard. You cut off two diagonally opposite squares, leaving 62 squares.

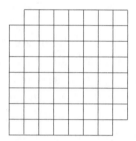

You have dominoes, each one covering two squares at once. The idea is to pave the surface (each domino must be *entirely* on the board; no part may stick out). Care to try it? [**Puzzle #22.** The solution is extremely elegant!]

• • •

The following story is true. The German mathematician Felix Klein was once at a party in which the company was discussing the correlation between music and mathematics—with respect to people's interests and abilities. Klein looked more and more puzzled and finally said, "But gentlemen, I don't understand! Mathematics is beautiful!"

I would like to also tell you two stories about the great German mathematician David Hilbert. He was very absent-minded and one evening, just as guests were about to arrive at his house for a

Lecturing,
Amherst 2002.

party, Hilbert's wife said to him: "David, go up and put on a nice tie." David went upstairs to his bedroom and didn't come down for an hour. His wife went upstairs to see what was wrong and found him asleep in bed. What happened was that once Hilbert took off his tie, he, by habit, took off the rest of his clothes and got into bed! [I find this story believable, because once when I changed my tie, I took off some of my clothes, but didn't go as far as getting into bed!]

Hilbert, though a fantastically brilliant mathematician had little practical common sense. His wife was the opposite. She had a great deal of practical common sense, but no mathematical ability. Someone once asked Hilbert whether his eighteen-year old son takes after him or his wife. Hilbert replied, "His mathematical ability he inherits from his mother. The rest he takes after me."

Speaking of mathematicians, I used to love to read incidents in the life of the weird Renaissance mathematician Cardan. He longed to know the secret of solving the cubic equation which was discovered by his contemporary, Tartaglia. He kept begging Tartaglia to tell him the secret, but to no avail. One day, he came to Tartaglia, and on his knees with tears in his eyes, begged and begged and swore the most solemn oaths that he would never, never reveal the secret to a single soul! Tartaglia relented and told him. The next day Cardan published the solution as his own!

At one point, Cardan got interested in astrology and cast his own horoscope, predicting the day he would die. When the day came, he committed suicide in order that his prediction be fulfilled.

• • •

I spoke to you earlier about Gödel numbering. There is a famous joke using a similar idea which has two endings, one of which is well-known and the other which is not, but I believe you will find the lesser known ending the funnier of the two.

The joke concerns a member of a "joke-makers' club" who invited a friend to one of their banquets. At the banquet, the friend was quite puzzled by the goings on—every now and then, someone would arise, call out a number and everyone else would laugh. When the friend asked what was going on, the host replied: "We joke-makers don't want to take the time to tell the whole joke, so we assign a number to each joke, and when the number of a joke is called, it calls to mind the joke, and we then laugh."

Now the well-known ending is this: The friend asks the host if he can try it, and the host assents. The friend rises, calls out a number, but no one laughs. When the friend asks the host why no one laughed, the host replied, "Some people can tell a joke and some cannot!"

The other ending, which I prefer, is this: A man gets up and calls out a very high number, everyone laughs and this one person keeps laughing much longer than everyone else. When the friend asked the host why that man was still laughing, the host replied: "He hasn't heard that one before."

• • •

I would now like to give you another illustration of the underlying logic of Gödel's proof. I put a quarter and a penny on the table and tell you that you should make a statement. If the statement is true, then I promise to give you one of the two coins, not saying which one, but if the statement is false, then I won't give you either coin. What statement could you make that would leave me no alternative but to give you the quarter? [Puzzle #23.]

I have also used the following more humorous illustration of Gödel's idea: Consider the following paradox:

THIS SENTENCE CAN NEVER BE PROVED.

The paradox is this: If the sentence is false, then what it says is *not* the case, which means that the sentence *can* be proved, but false sentences can't be proved. So if the sentence is false, we have a contradiction, so the sentence must be true.

Now, I have proven that the sentence is true. Since it is true, then what it says is really the case, which means that it can never be proved. So how come I just proved it?

What is the fallacy in the above reasoning? The fallacy is that the notion of *provable* is not well-defined. One purpose of the field of mathematical logic is to give a precise meaning to the word *proof*. Suppose, for example, that a student is taking a geometry exam and is asked to prove a certain theorem. The teacher returns the paper with the comment: "This is no proof!"

If the student were sophisticated, he could reply: "How do you know that what I have given is not a proof? You have not once defined *proof* in this course! You have defined things like angles and circles and other geometrical entities with admirable precision, but never have you defined *proof!* So how can you say that I have not given a *proof*. What *proof* do you have of this?"

As I said, mathematical logic *does* make the notion of proof a precise one. However, there has not yet been given a precise definition of *proof* in any absolute sense, but only *relative* to a given formal system. Now suppose we have a formal system—call it system *S*—in which the notion of *provability within the system S* is clearly defined. Suppose also that the system *S* is *correct* in the sense that it never proves any false sentences; every sentence provable in system *S* is true. Now consider the following sentence:

THIS SENTENCE IS NOT
PROVABLE IN SYSTEM S.

We now have no paradox, but an interesting truth instead: If the sentence were false, then the opposite of what it says would be the case—the sentence *would* be provable in system *S*, contrary to the given condition that no false sentences are provable in system S. Therefore, the sentence can't be false; it must be true. Hence what it asserts *is* the case—it is not provable in system S. Thus, the sentence is true but not provable in system S. This sentence is the informed counterpart of Gödel's sentence.

• • •

I must now tell you a cute incident: In my Chicago days, I knew a good pianist named Goodwin Sammel. He also had good mathematical ability and an excellent sense of humor. When I told him about Gödel's theorem, he straightaway composed the following dialogue:

A: It's true!

B: It's not!

A: Yes it is.

B: Prove it!

A: Oh, it can't be proved, but nevertheless it's true.

B: Now, just a minute. How can you say it's true if it can't be proved?

A: Oh, there are certain things that are true even though they can't be proved.

B: That's not true.

A: Yes, it is; Gödel *proved* that there are certain things that are true but cannot be proved.

B: That's not true!

A: Yes it is!

B: It couldn't be, and even if it were, it could never be proved!

• • •

Now, quite out of the blue, and for reasons you will soon understand, I wish to inform you that I am starting a new religion! Would you care to join? Like the Catholic Church, I have an Index of forbidden books—books you should not read. However, there is only one forbidden book in this Index. Can you guess what that book is? [**This is Puzzle #24.** I'll give you a hint: What I have in mind is close to paradoxical].

I love paradoxes! The solution to the last problem bears a similarity to the logician Quine's machine, which works only when it is out of operation.

I also like a paradox from the literary agent Lisa Collier, which she called *the business man's paradox:* The president of a certain firm offered a $100 reward to any employee who could suggest an idea that would save the company money. One of the employees suggested *eliminate the reward.*

The mathematician Stanislow Ulam once told me of something he thought of that he coined the *Nixon Paradox:* Shortly after Nixon's election to the presidency, he addressed his newly-formed cabinet and said, "Now, you are not *yes-men* are you? They all answered, "No!"

I am reminded of a cartoon I once saw in which a man was saying to his frightened servant: "I hate *yes-men,* Jeeves, don't you?"

Incidentally, is it possible for the words *yes* and *no* to be used synonymously? I can think of a context in which they are synonymous. Can you think of such a context? [**Puzzle #25.**]

I once thought of a cute little paradoxical story: A very bright kid says to his father: "Dad, suppose you visit Smullyan's island of liars and truth-tellers and meet a native who says to you, 'You will never know that I am a truth-teller.' What would you conclude?"

The father replies, "Well, son, I would reason this way: If he were a liar, his statement would be false which would mean that I *would* some time know that he is a truth-teller, but I can't *know* something that isn't so, hence he can't be a liar. He must be a truth-teller."

"Very good," says the boy, as he inwardly chuckled to himself. "So you would know that he is a truth-teller."

"Right. And since you would *know* he is a truth-teller, and it is impossible that a known thing can be wrong, then he really must be a truth-teller."

"Of course," replies the father.

"Then what he said must have been true."

"That's right."

"But this means that you never will know that he is a truth-teller, as he said! Yet you earlier said that you *do* know that he is a truth-teller. How come?"

"Oh, heavens!" says the father.

Actually, I myself once pulled such a mischievous trick on my dear unsuspecting wife. Once, at breakfast, I asked her, "Is *no* the correct answer to this question?"

"To what question?" she asked.

"To the question I just asked," I replied.

She thought for a moment and then said, "No, of course not!" I then said, "Aha! You answered *no* to the question, didn't you?" She agreed. "And did you answer correctly?" I asked.

"Of course," she replied.

"Then *no is* the correct answer to the question."

"Yes."

"Then when I asked you whether it was, you should have answered *yes,* not *no!* She thought for a moment and said, "I guess you're right. I should have said *yes* not *no.*"

"Oh," I said, "so *yes* is the correct answer to the question."

"That's right," she said.

I then said: "But if the correct answer is affirmative, as you just agreed, that means that *no* is the correct answer!"

"At which she said: "You're confusing me!" [Fortunately, she didn't divorce me over this].

The mathematician William Zwicker invented an interesting game called *Hypergame:* Call a game *normal* if it has to terminate after finitely many moves. Tic Tac Toe is obviously normal. Checkers is a normal game; so is chess with the 50 move rule. So are most card games. Now, the first move in Hypergame is to state

Taking it easy for a change.

which *normal* game is to be played. For example, suppose you and I are playing Hypergame and I have the first move. I might say, "Let's play chess," and you then make the first move in chess, and we continue playing chess until the game terminates. Or again, in my first move in Hypergame, I might say, "Let's play Tic Tac Toe," or "Let's play casino," or any other game I like. But the game I choose must be normal. I am not allowed to choose a game that is not normal.

Now, the problem is this: Is Hypergame itself normal or not? [**Puzzle #26.**]

• • •

I should sooner or later tell you something about computers, shouldn't I? The trouble is that I don't know anything about computers! I don't even have a word processor, because I can't even type. Like Martin Gardner, I am an old-fashioned scissors-and-paste man. No, I know nothing about computers. The funny thing, though, is that I have been told by computer scientists that some of my purely abstract work in mathematical logic has had applications to computer science, but I haven't the slightest idea of what these applications are! However, despite my lack of knowledge of computers, I do know some computer jokes!

The first is about a computer who was an expert about the stock market. Someone once programmed in the message: "How does one make money on stocks?" After much thought, the computer responded, *Buy low; sell high.*

Another computer was asked whether there was a God. After months of thought, the message came out: *There is now!*

Another computer was advertised as knowing everything! A salesman was demonstrating it to a customer and said: "Ask it anything, and it will answer you." The customer said, "O.K.," and asked the computer, "Where is my father?" The answer came out: ***YOUR FATHER IS NOW FISHING IN CANADA.***

The customer said, "You see, the machine is no good! It so happens that my father has been dead for many years!" The salesman said, "No, no, you must ask the machine in more precise language. Let me ask the question for you." The salesman then asked the computer: "Where is this man's mother's husband?" The answer came out:

HIS MOTHER'S HUSBAND HAS BEEN DEAD
FOR MANY YEARS. HIS FATHER IS NOW
FISHING IN CANADA.

Then there is the story of the military computer. When the army first sent a rocket to the moon, the colonel programmed into the computer two questions: (1) Will the rocket reach the moon? (2) Will the rocket return to earth? To the colonel's annoyance, the only answer that came back was YES. The colonel didn't know whether YES was the answer to the first question, or the second question, or the conjunction of the two questions, so he angrily programmed back? "Yes, what?" The machine responded, YES SIR!

A programmer and an engineer were sitting next to each other on a plane. The programmer asked the engineer if he would like to play a game. "No, I want to sleep," replied the engineer.

"It's a very interesting game!"

"No, no, I want to sleep."

"Look, the game is this: I ask you a question and if you don't know the answer, you pay me five dollars. Then, you ask me a question and if I don't know the answer, I pay you five dollars."

"No, no, I want to sleep."

"I'll tell you what," said the programmer, "if you don't know the answer to my question, you pay me five dollars, but if I don't know the answer to your question, I'll pay you fifty dollars!" The engineer thought for a moment and said, "All right," and then asked the programmer, "What goes up the hill with three legs and comes down with four?" The programmer took out his lap top computer and checked various references for an hour, but couldn't get the answer, hence he had to give fifty dollars to the engineer who said nothing but just put the fifty dollars into his pocket. The programmer, a bit miffed, said, "Well, what's the answer?" at which the engineer handed him five dollars.

• • •

Since I am a magician, as well as a logician, I like to combine logic and magic into what I call *logic tricks*. In fact some of my lectures were entitled *Logical Legerdemain*.

Suppose I hand you two ten-dollar bills and tell you that I am to make a statement. If the statement is false, then you are to hand me back one of the bills and keep the other, but if the statement is true, then you are to keep both bills. That sounds like a pretty good deal for you, doesn't it? Would you agree to this deal? If so, you shouldn't, because I could make a statement that the only way you could act as agreed would be to pay me a billion dollars! What statement would work? [**Puzzle #27.**]

I used the above trick once at a lecture to a group of mathematicians, and one of them took me up on the deal, hence owed me a billion dollars. I then said to him, "I'll tell you what. I'll give you a fifty percent chance of winning your billion dollars back, but for that I charge a nickel extra. Do you agree?" [This got a good laugh.] He agreed, and I wrote something on a piece of paper, folded it up and handed it to someone else to hold for me to prevent any possibility of my using any sleight of hand. I then said, "I've written on the paper a certain event that may or may not take place in this room within the next fifteen minutes. You are to guess whether it will or will not take place. If you guess correctly, then I will give you back the billion dollars you owe me, otherwise I won't."

I then walked over to him with a pen and a blank piece of paper and said, "If you believe the event will take place, write *yes,* and if you believe the event won't take place, write *no.*" I then walked back to the lectern and asked him: "Have you written your answer?" He replied that he had. I then said, "Then you have lost!" You see, what I wrote was such that regardless of whether he wrote *yes* or *no,* he would be wrong. What could I have written that would accomplish this? [**Puzzle #28.** This is a cute trick that any of you can do!]

At that point he owed me a billion dollars. Well, I was in a very generous mood at the time, and so I said, "I'll tell you what. I think I'll give you back the billion dollars, and even the extra nickel, as a gift and claim a tax deduction."

At another lecture, I showed that I had two envelopes and explained that in one of them was a dollar bill and the other one was empty. I then explained, "Anyone who agrees to play this game with me, if you can determine which envelope contains the bill, you can have it. To enable you to make the determination, each envelope has a sentence written on the outside. From that sentence, you are to deduce which envelope contains the bill. It is not enough for you to *guess* which envelope has the bill, you must be able to *prove* that it does before the envelope is opened. For the privilege of doing this, I charge a quarter. Is anyone game?"

I then showed the two envelopes:

(1) THE SENTENCES ON BOTH ENVELOPES ARE BOTH FALSE.	*(2) THE BILL IS IN THE OTHER ENVELOPE.*

Can you figure out which envelope contains the bill? Why don't you try it out before reading further?

One of the group volunteered to play the game with me. After thinking for a moment, he said: "The bill must be in Envelope #1."

"What is your proof?" I asked.

He replied: "Obviously, the sentence on Envelope #1 must be false, because if it were true, both sentences would be false, which is absurd. Hence Sentence #1 is false. Since it is false, then what it says is not the case—it is not the case that both sentences are false, hence one of them must be true, and since Sentence #1 is not true, it must be Sentence #2 that is true, which means that the bill is in Envelope #1, as the sentence says."

"That sounds logical," I said. "Now open up the envelopes." He opened up the Envelope #1 and found it empty. He then opened Envelope #2, and there was the bill! What was wrong with his reasoning? [**Puzzle #29.**]

Eastern Philosophy

My nine puzzle books are full of puzzles of the type I have described. These books have been quite successful and have received excellent reviews and have been translated into eighteen languages. In addition to these nine books and my six technical books on logic and set theory, I have published three others of a totally different nature. It happened in the following way:

In 1969 I got very interested in Eastern philosophy, particularly in Zen Buddhism. I once humorously defined Zen as a mixture of Chinese Taoism and Indian Buddhism with a touch of pepper and salt, particularly pepper thrown in by the Japanese.

I observed some interesting parallels between some Zen stories and some Jewish stories. For example, in one Zen story, a monk went up the mountain to interview a Zen master, who asked him whether he came from the North or the South. The monk told him that he came from the South, at which the Master said: "In that case, have a cup of tea." The next day, another monk came up the mountain and when asked, told the Master that he came from the North, at which the Master said: "In that case, have a cup of tea." Later on the Master's assistant said to him, "I don't understand! To the one who came for the South, you told him to have a cup of tea, and to the one from the North, you also told him to have a cup of tea. Why?"

The master replied, "Have a cup of tea."

The Jewish counterpart is the story of two women, Mrs. Cohen and Mrs. Goldberg, who were arguing over the ownership of a chicken. They could not settle it, and so they decided to give the problem to the rabbi. The rabbi first privately interviewed Mrs. Cohen, and after hearing her version said, "I agree with you, Mrs. Cohen; you are absolutely right!" Later, the rabbi heard Mrs. Goldberg's case and said, "I agree with you, Mrs. Goldberg; you are absolutely right!"

After both ladies left, the rabbi's wife, who had heard both interviews, said to her husband, "Now look, the two can't *both* be right! If Mrs. Cohen is right, then Mrs. Goldberg is wrong, and if Mrs. Goldberg is right, then Mrs. Cohen must be wrong. They can't both be right!" To which the rabbi replied: "I agree with you, dear; you're absolutely right!"

• • •

After studying Zen for a few months, I realized it was more the Taoistic elements than the Buddhist elements that appealed to me, so I set to work writing my book, *The Tao Is Silent* (Harper and Row), a series of essays and short stories inspired by Taoistic ideas. The reactions to this book have been surprisingly mixed. A review by the *Library Journal* begins, "Readers will either love this book or hate this book," which is not too surprising.

More surprising are the following two dramatically opposed attitudes: One Zen Master wrote me a letter informing me that I had the subject all wrong, and that if I wished to obtain enlightenment and see into my own nature, I should consult his teacher.

On the other hand, a Japanese philosopher teaching at Princeton told me this was the best book on Taoism that he had ever read in either English or Japanese. So whom should I believe? Many loved the playful spirit of the book; others criticized my approach to Taoism as too playful. Actually, I regard Taoism as both playful and profound. What does the word *Tao* mean? It is difficult to define. The only way one can get a good feeling for its meaning is to see the word used in hundreds of contexts. The word has overtones of *God, Nature, Reason, The Way, The reason things are the way they are,* and many other things. I could name more. To me personally, Taoism represents a state of serenity combined with a state of intense aesthetic awareness.

Let me give you an example of one of my "playful" approaches in the book.

On The Art of Management

Chuangtse has a marvelous passage in which (in the words of Lin Yutang) he discusses the idea of preserving man's original nature by comparing the harm done to that nature by the Confucians and the harm done to a horse by a famous horse-trainer.

> *Horses have hoofs to carry them over frost and snow, and hair to protect them from wind and cold. They feed on grass and drink water, and fling up their tails and gallop. Such is the real nature of horses. They have no use for ceremonial halls and big dwellings.*
>
> *One day Polo (famous horse-trainer) appeared, saying, "I am good at managing horses." So he burned their hair and clipped them, and pared their hoofs and branded them. He put halters around their necks and shackles around their legs and numbered them according to their stables. The result was that two or three in every ten died. Then he kept them hungry and thirsty, trotting them and galloping them, and taught them to run in formation, with the misery of the tasselled bridle in front of them and the fear of the knotted whip behind, until more than half of them died.*
>
> *The potter says, ""I am good at managing clay. If I want it round, I use compasses; if rectangular, a square." The carpenter says, ""I am good at managing wood. If I want it curved, I use an arc; if straight, a line." But on what grounds can we think that the nature of clay and wood desires this application of compasses and square, and arc and line? Nevertheless, every age extolls Polo for his skill in training horses, and potters and carpenters for their skill with clay and wood.*

Some Interesting Memories

Those who manage (govern) the affairs of the empire make the same mistake...

I read this passage to Vincent, a teen-age relative; he loved it as much as I did. Several days later one of my dogs had to be taken to the vet. It was a beautiful spring day, and we walked the dog on a grassy terrace just outside the office. The dog, seeing the office and having been there before, was trembling like a leaf. Several other dogs were there being walked by their owners, and they were all trembling like leaves. At this point Vincent glanced in the direction of the office, glanced back at me, and said, "I see he knows how to manage dogs."

• • •

I must tell you a remarkable story about this book, that sounds like a joke, but really isn't: A Scotsman, who read the book, wrote me, "I very much enjoyed your book *The Tao is Silent,* and I'm even thinking of buying a copy."

• • •

This book on Taoism began my career as an essayist. Two other books of essays soon followed: *Five Thousand B. C. and Other Philosophical Fantasies* and *This Book Needs No Title.* The former bears the same sort of relation to philosophy as science fiction bears to science, although one philosopher told me that in saying this, I am underrating its philosophical significance.

The book has been translated into German, as well as other languages, and a native German philosopher who had read it in both English and German amused me by saying: "You sound more profound in German than in English. I guess everybody does."

As a sample of the spirit of *This Book Needs No Title,* I have the story of two men, one of whom asks the other whether he is happy or unhappy at the moment. When told that he is *both,* the other asks for an explanation. The other then says, "I have just heard the first really convincing proof of the immortality of the soul. Now I know that I will survive my bodily death, which makes me very happy. On the other hand, my steak is overdone."

GOD • Religion

I have also written on religious themes. During my childhood, I had absolutely no religious training, thank God! The reason I say "thank God" is that I am extremely grateful that I was never indoctrinated as a child. Any views I hold are the result of my own reading and thinking. Many years ago, a psychiatrist told me that no intelligent person could ever believe in God. I reminded him that a mutual friend whom he described as the most intelligent person he had ever known, other than himself, was in fact a devout Catholic.

I also told him that it was not a sign of lack of intelligence to have to follow a post-hypnotic suggestion. He agreed that holding beliefs instilled during childhood is quite similar to following post-hypnotic suggestion.

I do not believe that the belief in some sort of God is due to indoctrination, but do believe that adherence to any of the world's religions is. I agree with those religionists who say that Nature suggests a God, but fail to see that Nature suggests that God wrote any of the Bibles. Indeed, it seems to me that the difference between atheism and the belief in God is extremely small compared to the difference between belief in God and the belief that God wrote any of the Bibles! I believe that any completely unprejudiced person would believe that *some* intelligence is or has been operative, but belief in any of the world's religions is a very different story. I recall an amusing theological conversation I once had with a friend in which I asked him whether he believed in God. He said, "I certainly believe in *something.*" I replied, "I also believe in something, only I do not know what that something is! He replied: "Same with me."

I do not subscribe to any religions though, I do believe that some intelligence is responsible for life. The idea that life has evolved *by* chance seems to me, not impossible, but totally implausible. What this intelligence is, I have no idea, nor have I any way of knowing whether this intelligence is conscious or not. Nor do I have any way of knowing whether or not this intelligence still exists. Is this equivalent to considering the possibility that God is dead?

I have always hated the phrase "God is dead" and regarded it as most misleading. I think that the word "dead" should be applied only to formerly living biological organisms. I see no reason to believe that whatever intelligence has been responsible for all this is necessarily still operative. There are so many possibilities! It could be that the intelligence has split up into the consciousness of all living beings. It could be that it has gone off into another space-time continuum. Or it could be that the physical universe itself might be that intelligence—a giant computer, for all we know.

Although I do not subscribe to any of the world's religions, I am not *against* them, as are some people I know. I am indeed strongly against *some* ideas in *some* of the world's religions—ideas that strike me as absolutely barbaric! I won't say what these ideas are, nor what religions hold them, since I don't want to hurt anyone's feelings. In general, I am very interested in *comparative* religion. I'd like to try to find out what underlying truth there may be behind all of the world's religions.

To me, one of the wisest things ever said about religion was said by Ralph Waldo Emerson in his *Journal*. Although he mentions the Swedenborgians specifically, his remarks seem to me to be perfectly applicable to *all* religions. Here is what he says:

> *October 9, 1829: I am glad to see that interpretations of Scriptures like those of the New Jerusalem Church (The church of Swedenborg) can be accepted in our community. The most spiritual and sublime sense is put upon various historical passages of the New Testament. The interpretation is doubtless wholly false. The Apostle John and our Saviour meant no such things. But the sentiment which the commentator puts into their mouths is nevertheless true and eternal. The wider that sentiment can be spread, and the more effect it can have on men's lives, the better. And if the fool-part of man must have the lie, if truth is a pill that can't go down*

*till it is sugared with superstition, why then I will forgive
the last, in the belief that truth will enter the soul so natively
and assimilantly that it will become part of the soul, and so
remain when the falsehood grows dry and peels off.*

He has said in a more graphic, poetic and convincing way than
anything I have ever seen before, something I have long believed—
namely that all the religions, though full of myths, falsehoods and
superstitions, are nevertheless all converging toward the truth.

I once thought of the following parable: Three men were standing in a field. One of them said, "Look at the elephant way over
there!" A second one said: "That's not an elephant, it's a hippopotamus!" Well, the two argued back and forth, and finally asked
the third man what he saw it as, to which the man replied: "I can't
see it at all; I'm blind."

To me, the atheist is blind, whereas the religionist is sighted,
but his vision is distorted. I believe that all of the existing religions are full of falsehoods, but they are dynamic and progressing
and nearer to the truth than atheism, which is static and going
nowhere.

The one religious philosophy that has appealed to me most is
that of Richard Bucke in his remarkable book *Cosmic Consciousness* (E.P. Dutton, 1901). About this book, Professor H. A. Overstreet, formerly of the Department of Philosophy and Psychology of the College of the City of New York said in his interesting
book, *The Enduring Quest* (W. W. Norton & Company) the following about Bucke's book:

*In the year 1901, a remarkable book was published by a Ca-
nadian physician and psychiatrist of wide reading and pen-
etrative originality... And yet it is significant to note that
in the thirty years since Bucke published his remarkable work,
practically nothing has been done in the investigation of the
idea which he suggested. Nevertheless this idea is so obviously important that it would seem to merit instant atten-*

tion. It is the idea that, inasmuch as evolution of life-forms (including the psychological) continues, we have every reason to believe that a further form of our conscious life is already observable among us—in high degree among rare individuals, in lesser degree among most of us. The full emergencies into that further form, Bucke suggests, would naturally not be instantaneous—the whole of humanity leaping, so to speak, into a new order of being. As in all the stages of evolution, we should expect slight difference in one more happily circumstanced individual, then in a few others, then in more, until finally the new form would become widespread and secure. What he proposed is that we look about to see whether there are any outstanding examples among us of a form of conscious life which might properly be regarded as of a higher order than that with which we are familiar. This, he suggested, would not be a form totally discontinuous with our normal consciousness, but one which would already be adumbrated in the more significant process of our mental and emotional life.

Speaking of the great people whom Bucke cited as cases of Cosmic Consciousness, Overstreet says:

Wherein lay the secret of their superiority? That is the problem to which Bucke addresses himself. His answer, whether true or false—and we must remember that his book was a pioneering venture—is sufficiently arresting to call for our serious consideration. Studying the life histories of these men, he finds in all of them—sometimes in great degree, sometimes in less—a clearly marked phenomenon of consciousness. These men do not reason—the search for truth—apparently played a part in preparation for their final insight. In every case they experienced what, for want of a better term, we might call illumination.

It is significant that Bucke subtitled his book "A Study of the Evolution of the Human Mind." Briefly, Cosmic Consciousness, according to Bucke, is a higher form of consciousness that is slowly but surely coming to the entire human race *through the process of evolution.* The mystics and religious leaders of the past were simply ahead of their time—they were *evolutionary sports.* Bucke believes that Cosmic Consciousness is the *real* source of all the world's religions. He did not believe that the cosmic state is necessarily infallible. Like the development of any faculty, it takes a long time to become perfected. And so, just because Cosmic Consciousness is the *root* of religious beliefs, it doesn't follow that the beliefs are necessarily correct. One thing I particularly like about Bucke's approach is that it is totally non-authoritarian. He believes that when Cosmic Consciousness comes fully to the entire human race, everyone will then *directly* perceive that which was formerly believed only on authority. That is, the Cosmic Sense is not dependent on any *belief* in authority; it carries its own authority, in the same way that our normal senses do.

The bulk of Bucke's book is devoted to an analysis of the writings of many religious leaders, philosophers, writers and poets whom he believes to have had Cosmic Consciousness. The reason I believe this book to be of such great value is that even if there is no metaphysical significance to Bucke's idea, even if his magnificently prophetic vision is only a beautiful pipe dream, his book should be considered significant to even the most skeptical readers, because the analysis and comparison of the quoted writings is of enormous psychological, philosophical, aesthetic and literary interest. [For example, his analysis of some of the Shakespearean sonnets puts them in a very different light, as does his analysis of some of the religious writings.] The reader will certainly sense something in common with all these writings, and what this is may aptly be called the *Cosmic Sense.*

Someone, realizing my enthusiasm for this book, asked me if *I* had Cosmic Consciousness. I replied that I believe that Cosmic Consciousness is a matter of degree, that everyone has *some* degree of Cosmic Consciousness—just as everyone has *some* musical *sense* and *some* sense of humor. In some, it may exist in such a faint degree as to be barely recognizabile. Others may have it to a slightly higher degree, but out of skepticism may repress the knowledge that they have it. I find it amusing that when Bucke told Walt Whitman that he had Cosmic Consciousness, Whitman seemed unimpressed and shrugged his shoulders in a good-natured way, as if to say: "If it makes you happy to think of it that way, by all means do so!" Bucke, who believed that Whitman had Cosmic Consciousness to an extreme degree said about him: "Walt Whitman, in my talks with him at that time, always disclaimed any lofty intention in himself or his poems. If you accepted his explanations, they were simple and commonplace. But when you came to think about these explanations, and to enter into the spirit of them, you found that the simple and commonplace with him involved the ideal and the spiritual."

Speaking of Walt Whitman, one of my favorite incidents about him was related by Logan Pearsall Smith (the brother-in-law of Bertrand Russell) in his book *Unforgotten Years* (Little Brown and Company, 1939). The author's sister Alys (who was the first wife of Bertrand Russell) in her college years was enamored of Whitman's writings and once told her father that she planned to pay Whitman a visit. The father was furious and said, "No daughter of mine is going to visit a dissolute character like that! Well, after a bout of arguing, the father realized that his daughter had a strong will of her own and that the case was hopeless. And so he said, "Well, you're not going to go alone! Your brother and I will go with you!" She said "fine," and the three drove off in their carriage and paid a visit to the old bard. Well, Whitman was very affable and loquacious. The father was at first morosely silent, but gradually warmed up to Whitman and ended up inviting Whitman to drive home with them and have dinner. Whitman put on his hat, drove home with them, had dinner, and remained a guest in their house for a whole month! [That's what I call a reasonable father!]

Some years ago, I went into a bookstore in New York and asked the lady if she had any material on Walt Whitman. She replied: "As a matter of fact, *you* remind me of Walt Whitman. I guess many people have told you that before." I replied, "No one has ever told me that I remind *you* of Walt Whitman!"

More School Days

Coming back to my Princeton days, after two years, I passed the general exams and was appointed an instructor. During my third year, I wrote my Ph.D. dissertation at the same time that I taught. At the end of the third year, I took my last examination and passed. Right after that, some fellow graduate students asked me, "Do you now want us to call you 'Doctor'?" I, who have never taken titles seriously, could not refrain from drawing myself up stiffly and sternly saying, "I want you to call me *field marshal!*

I taught a second year at Princeton and then taught at several other universities. At one point I was invited to give some lectures at the University of Texas at Austin, where I was being considered for an appointment. I was interviewed by several departmental chairmen, all but one of whom treated me with courtesy and respect. But one chairman seemed quite hostile to me as soon as we met and almost immediately after, said to me in an angry tone: "What evidence do I have that you're a good teacher? Now look, I don't want anyone involved in their egocentric research; I want people who can teach! How do I know you are a good teacher? I don't want any egocentric researchers! Now, you see that certificate on the wall over there? That proves that *I* am a good teacher!"

I could not but inwardly smile at the man's incredible egocentricity, but what I told him was that with me, teaching and research have always been thoroughly integrated. One of my main research interests is finding simpler and more elegant proofs of various results, and this of course, is most useful in teaching. As one graduate student told me, she particularly loved an advanced course I had given, largely because it was obvious to her that I was doing research on the topics I was teaching.

Incidentally, I know that I am known to be an exceptionally

good teacher, though some of my more unorthodox methods have been a source of exasperation to some of my colleagues, particularly the fact that I am an unusually easy grader. I am far more interested in getting a student to love a subject than to learn a lot about it, though in pursuing this ideal, the student usually *does* learn a lot! I love the little-known saying of Confucius about education: "To learn is not as good as to love." I wish more educators would realize that the only valid discipline of a subject comes from the student's interest in it; it should not come from any other source. My policy is to teach the student as much as possible and to require from him or her as little as possible. I was particularly gratified when a student once told me: "Professor Smullyan, I am puzzled! You seem to demand nothing from us. You don't insist on our doing our homework. We all know that you are a most easy-grader, yet many of us have told me that they have never worked so hard in any course in their lives! I am one of them."

My method of grading elementary courses is surely unorthodox but I believe, has been very successful. I encourage lots of class participation and soon get to know the quality of each student. At the end of the semester, instead of giving a final exam, I interview each student separately and ask him or her to tell me honestly what grade he thinks he deserves. I explain that I have already made my estimate of the appropriate grade, and the rule will be this: If our two estimates are the same, that's it. If his estimate is lower than mine, then I give him the higher of the two estimates. If his estimate is higher than mine, then we discuss the matter further [and we usually compromise with some intermediate grade]. Now what's interesting is that in the majority of cases, our estimates have been identical. Still more interesting is that in almost all cases in which our estimates were different, the student's estimate was *lower* than mine!

I have taught groups ranging from remedial students to advanced graduate students. My experience teaching remedial students was really an eye opener! For example, many of the students were surprised to learn that when an object was divided into two equal parts, each part was half of the whole! Also, I once asked a class if seven inches are cut off of a piece of string a hundred inches long, how much is left? To my surprise, they couldn't get it. When I told them that the answer was ninety-three, one of them said: "Oh, you get that by *subtraction!*" The amazing thing is that if I had asked them how much is one hundred minus seven, they would have gotten it, but they had no idea of how subtraction applied to the physical world!

To these students, I always tried to emphasize how mathematics was related to common sense. As an amusing example: When I once gave an exam in algebra, I gave a typical problem involving finding the ages of a mother, father and child. I told the class, "For this problem, I'll give you a hint." All eyes turned to me eagerly. I said, "If the child should turn out to be older than either parent, then you've done something wrong."

I often present material in novel ways. For example, to explain the Pythagorean theorem, I draw a right triangle on the board and draw squares on the hypotenuse and sides and tell the students, "Imagine these three squares are made of valuable gold leaf and that you are given the option of taking either the one big square or the two little ones, which would you choose?" Usually about half the class opts for the one big square and half for the two smaller ones, and both groups are equally amazed when I prove that it makes no difference!

To further imprint Pythagoras' theorem on their minds, I usually tell the story of the American Indian chief who had three squaws. One slept on the hide of a bear, one on the hide of a deer, and one on the hide of a hippopotamus—sort of status symbols. After a while, the squaw on the hide of the bear had a daughter, the squaw on the hide of the deer had a son, and the squaw on the hide of the hippopotamus had twins, which proves that the squaw on the hide of the hippopotamus is equal to the sum of the squaws on the other two hides. [All right, all right!]

To those students who have to take exams, let me give the following advice: Never spend any time at all on any one question, as this will take time away from the others!

I once did give an exam in freshman calculus, and some of my questions, though ingenious, were perhaps a bit too difficult. To my amusement, one of the students looked up at me and said, "Proud of yourself?"

Once I was proctoring an exam given by another teacher. My purpose was to see that no one was cheating. I said to the class, "Will you give me your word of honor that you won't cheat if I give you mine that I won't report you if you do?"

Incidentally, if you wish to cheat on exams, I have a good suggestion of how to do so. One person simply gets up and yells out all the answers, and this will be so obvious that nobody will ever suspect anything!

Now, some advice for those who *give* examinations. Be sure of writing at the head of the exam:

"CORRECT ANSWERS GET MORE CREDIT THAN INCORRECT ONES."

Also, remember that the best day of the year to give an examination is February 30.

I love the story of an examination in which at one point the proctor said, "The examination is closed. Stop writing!" Well, one boy wrote for 30 seconds longer, and when he took his paper to the desk, all the other papers had been handed in. The proctor said: "I can't accept your paper; you cheated! You wrote overtime." The boy drew himself up stiffly and in a proud voice said, "Do you know *who* I am? The proctor replied, "No." The boy said, "Good!" and stuck his paper in the stack of papers and quickly walked away.

THE *Purple Tree* PRESENTS
RAYMOND MERRILL

A magic brochure.

Hobbies and Horsing Around

Back to my own life. In addition to my writing, teaching, lecturing, "magicking," piano playing and generally horsing around, I have had many fascinating hobbies. In my high school days, I made telescopes and observed the heavenly bodies. I first used long-focus eyeglass lenses as objectives, and later I bought many war-supply achromats for objectives. Then, I joined the Amateur Astronomers Association at the American Museum of Natural History. There I ground and polished and figured a six-inch mirror and I soon got accepted into the Optical Division. I then got interested in stereo photography, and using a Stereo Realist camera, made a lovely collection of stereo slides of one of my European trips.

Another hobby: stereoscopy.

Later on, I became interested in a larger format—60 mm. I have constructed about thirty odd viewers for stereo slides that are optically far superior to any that are commercially available (though they are mechanically not as refined), and I have published an article about them in the publication *Stereoscopy.*

In one stage of my life, I collected many used books at relatively low cost. Indeed, I picked up at a library a copy of Kant's *Critique of Pure Reason* for 5 cents. When I told this to a logician, he told me, "I think you grossly overpaid!" [Are you familiar with Mark Twain's definition of a good library? According to him, a good library doesn't have to have any books. All that's required is that it has no books by Jane Austen.]

I am also an avid collector of LP records and have built cabinets to house them. My latest hobby has been hi-fi audio stereo. I have put together six hi-fi systems in my house, the most inter-

Some stereoscopic viewers I have made.

esting of which is in my upstairs study and uses 40 speakers. Yes, 40 speakers! Expensive? Not at all. They are used speakers purchased at yard sales and Salvation Army stores. Individually, most of them are not all that good, but blended together in the right way, the results are remarkable! For example, if one speaker has too much treble and one has too much bass, if the two are blended together, they may sound just right.

Generally, in large groups of speakers, errors of various ones tend to cancel each other out. How does one blend 40 speakers together? Well, look at it this way: The average speaker has an impedance of 8 ohms. Put two of them in series, and the combination has an impedance of 16 ohms. Now, put together two others in series for another 16-ohm combination. Then, if these two pairs are put together in parallel, we are back to 8 ohms. Thus, 4 eight-ohm speakers can be put in a series-parallel combination and will then function as a single 8-ohm speaker. One can similarly put 4 such foursomes into a parallel-series combination and then have 16 speakers acting like one 8-ohm speaker. Indeed, I could have used only one amplifier to drive all 40 speakers without any more strain than if it had driven just two 8-ohm speakers, but I prefer to divide my speakers into four groups and use 4 amplifiers, one for each group, because each group has its own tonal characteristics. Then I have control over the individual volumes of each of the groups and blend them together in a variety of ways. Hi-fi experts who have heard my system have marveled at the quality of sound. I thought that my idea was original, until I heard that there is a commercial system available that used 60 speakers. However, this commercial system sells for eighty-thousand dollars! My set of speakers cost me a little over $300.

Joking Around

Before when I said "horsing around," I was thinking partly of the various pranks I have played in my life—particularly in my student days. My favorite one was when I would have a date and ask the girl if she believed it to be possible to kiss a girl without touching her. When she said it was obviously not, I would bet her that I could. When she bet me that I couldn't, I would ask her to close her eyes and would then give her a kiss and say, "I lose!" [I like that so much better than the grade school joke of saying: "I bet I can punch you without hurting you."]

A significant variant of this joke occurred in my third year as a graduate student at Princeton. I frequently visited New York in those days, and I met a charming lady musician who directed an excellent music school. On our first date, I asked her to do me a favor. I was to make a statement and asked her to give me her autograph if the statement were true. She saw no reason why not. I then said, "If my statement is false, then you agree *not* to give me your autograph." She assented. And so the idea was that a true statement gets an autograph and a false statement does not. Well, I then made a statement such that to keep our agreement, she had to give me, not her autograph, but a kiss! What statement would work? [**Puzzle #30.**]

Next, instead of collecting the kiss, I suggested that we play double-or-nothing, to which she agreed. She soon owed me two kisses, then four, then eight, and things kept doubling and doubling and escalating and escalating. The end result? We got married! We have now been married for forty-three years.

With Blanche for 43 years!

• • •

An incident now comes to my mind that is very close to my heart—an incident about the famous former opera singer, Lauritz Melchior. Sometime in the twenties, Melchior was sitting in the back yard of his house in Germany when an amazing thing happened: At the time there was a very popular actress in Germany who was known as the Mary Pickford of Germany.

One time she was making a moving picture and had to parachute out of a plane. The wind blew the parachute off course, and she landed right in Lauritz Melchior's back yard, almost in his arms. Three days later, they were engaged! You see, I am very much a romanticist at heart [as well as a classicist] and am delighted with the idea of a wife dropping out of the sky!

Another incident that appeals to my romantic heart is one I heard as a child. A burglar once came into a house, and when he entered, he heard a little girl playing the piano so beautifully that he was moved to tears. Instead of robbing the house, he gave the girl a lovely ring and departed.

Speaking of intruders, a psychiatrist once told me the following true incident: One of his female patients once dreamed that she heard a strange man come into the house and slowly walk up the stairs towards her bedroom. She was frightened out of her wits! He finally opened the door, went over to her bed and stared at her. She said in a terrified voice, "What are you going to do now?" He replied: "That depends on you, lady; this is *your* dream!"

This same psychiatrist had a male patient who told her the following, "Last night, I had an interesting dream. I was on the verge of committing suicide and you knew about it. To divert me, you pretended to be drowning. I rushed out to save you and completely forget about my own suicide. How clever of you!"

"Yes," replied the psychiatrist, "it was clever of you."

"No, no!" said the patient, "It was clever of *you*, not *me!*"

The psychiatrist replied: "It was *your* dream, not mine."

Incidentally, Freud was once asked whether a man should be held responsible for what he dreamed. Freud replied: "Whom else would you hold responsible?"

My favorite psychiatrist joke is about a man who went to a psychiatrist with the following problem. When he lay in bed at night, he was afraid somebody might be under the bed, so he went under the bed. Then he was afraid that somebody was on top of the bed, so he went back on top, but then was afraid that someone might be underneath. He kept alternating all night between the top of the bed and underneath, and got no sleep. The psychiatrist told him that his problem was curable, but that he would have to come five times a week for three years at a hundred-and-fifty dollars a session. The man said he would have to think about it and left. A few months later, the psychiatrist met the man on the street and asked him what he had decided. The man replied, "My problem has already been solved. I told it to my bartender and he said for ten dollars, he would give me a solution, and the solution worked perfectly!"

"What was the solution?" asked the psychiatrist.

The man replied: "He told me to saw off the legs."

I also like the story of a little girl who wouldn't come out from under her bed. Nothing the parents could do would get her out, so they called a psychiatrist to the house. After spending some time in the girl's bedroom, he came out looking very grave. The parents asked him what was wrong. "Well," said the psychiatrist," this is a very strange case. She has the idea that if she should ever venture out of her hiding place, people around would start biting her!"

Oh, is that all?" said the mother. "In that case, I guess we ought to stop biting her."

• • •

Let me now say a little about my teaching career. After my two years teaching at Princeton, I taught at New York University, SUNY at New Paltz, Vassar College, Belfer Graduate School of Science, CUNY Lehman College and Graduate Center, and finally Indiana University at Bloomington in the Philosophy Department, holding the Oscar Ewing chair.

Indiana University

It is interesting how I came to Indiana. The famous computer scientist Douglas Hofstadter, who wrote the extremely popular and informative book *Gödel, Escher and Bach,* had read a good deal of my writings. He liked *The Tao Is Silent,* and particularly the dialogue in it between a mortal and God concerning the question of free will. [In it, I pictured God as a *therapist,* rather than a ruler.] Douglas also liked my puzzle books, and was especially interested in my popularization of Gödel's theorem. As a result, he invited me to come and give some lectures at Indiana University, which I accepted. There I met Professor Michael Dunn, who was then chairman of the Philosophy department. He had read a good deal of my technical work and expressed interest in my coming to Indiana University permanently, which I did. My position there was the most interesting one I had ever had!

I had lots of fun there with Hofstadter, but first let me tell you of an interesting philosophical disagreement we had (and still have) about a positive version of a problem known as the *Prisoner's Dilemma,* of which numerous articles have been written. Suppose that you and I are to play a game, a sponsor of which will give us a little money for the interest of seeing us play it. Each of us is to do one of two things, titled *cooperation* and *defection.* If we both defect, we each get one dollar. If we both cooperate, we each get three dollars from the sponsor. If we both defect, defector gets five dollars and the cooperfator gets nothing! What is your best strategy, to cooperate or defect?

Well, if I should cooperate, you will get more by defecting than cooperating—namely five dollars versus three dollars. If I should defect, you will gain more by defecting than cooperating—namely one dollar versus nothing. Thus in either case you will gain more by defecting than by cooperating. Therefore, you should defect. And so we both defect, and we each get one dollar, whereas if we had both cooperated, we would each have received three dollars! Isn't that strange?

Well, how should we act? Here is where Doug and I disagree.

from a *moral* point of view, I would cooperate. But if I played purely selfishly, if I wanted to *maximize* my gain, I would defect. But Douglas believed that, leaving morality completely aside, and playing from a purely *selfish* point of view, one should cooperate. His argument was that the two of us were rational beings, and each of us knows that the other one is rational, and therefore will realize that the two of us will play alike. Well, of course if I were certain that we would play alike, then I would cooperate, but I see no reason to believe that we would necessarily play alike. Yes, if you and I, that is, the two who are playing the game, were allowed to communicate beforehand, then of course we would both agree to cooperate, but we are not allowed to do this, and so I see no reason to believe that we will play alike. Still, Doug believes that we, as rational beings, will play alike.

Douglas actually got *Scientific American* to sponsor this game, in which each participant played against all the others. We were asked to play *selfishly*, not morally. Needless to say, the defectors won more, and so I would say were the more rational ones. Yet Douglas has raised an interesting point, and there is really much more to this seemingly paradoxical situation than meets the eye!

As I said before, Doug and I had great fun together at the University. We gave several presentations together, in some of which we acted out portions of dialogues from each of our books. Doug is a very good actor, and we both had our audiences highly amused. We also had some public philosophical debates, he taking a more or less materialistic position and I, and idealistic one. At one point I suggested that we each take the other's position and argue for it, to which Doug agreed. At the time I was in a particularly mischievous mood, and I lashed into Doug full force and yelled: "Ah yes, you with your long white hair and overgrown beard and with your nonsensical mystical ideas, you're probably getting *senile*, that's what it is!" This got Doug so cracked up with laughter that he couldn't answer!

April Fools' Day

Ah yes, we had great fun! I also had great fun with many others at the University—faculty and students alike. I must tell you one very amusing incident about Mike Dunn's two children—Johnny, aged 8 and Jennifer, aged 6. One April Fools' Day Johnny came down the stairs and played an April Fools' joke on his parents. Half an hour later little Jennifer came down and Johnny tried an April Fool's joke on her at which she responded, "What the matter with you Johnny, today's not April Fool!" Surprised, he replied, "It isn't?" Upon which she said, "April Fool." That's what I would call a "meta-April Fools' joke."

I really love April Fools' jokes. One of the favorite ones I like to play is to phone someone on April 1st and in the course of the conversation say, "Did you read that fantastic article in *The New York Times* today about Leonardo da Vinci? You didn't? It's hard to believe, but there is absolutely incontrovertible evidence that da Vinci was really a woman! Impossible you say? I'm telling you the evidence is now absolutely conclusive. By the way, what is the date today?"

I pulled this joke a few days ago on an assistant to Bob Long, the editor and publisher of this book. Her name is Jeanne, and when I asked to speak to Bob she announced that Bob was out at the moment. I then pulled the joke and when I came to the point where I asked what the date was, she suddenly realized it was an April Fools' joke, and said, "You're bad!" Later she got even with me when I called back and asked her to please let me speak to Bob. She recognized my voice and said, "You have the wrong number." When I said, "I'm sorry," she replied, "April Fool!"

Another great April Fools' joker is Martin Gardner. He is also an excellent magician. Every couple of years a gathering in Atlanta is organized by Tom Rodgers in Martin's honor, in which many magicians have performed.

One of my favorite magicians is Michael Weber, a lawyer from San Francisco. He did two particularly noteworthy tricks: The first he played on me at a dining room table and is the best card trick I have ever seen! I selected a card from a shuffled deck, signed my name on the back, and returned it to the deck, which was then shuffled. He took the deck, looked through it and said he couldn't find what he thought was my card, and asked me if I could find it. I took the deck, looked through it and was also unable to find the card. At that point a waiter came in from the kitchen bearing my card with my signature on the back! Not bad, eh?

The second of my favorites of Michael's tricks was done before a large audience at the gathering and was particularly humorous: He had three ladies come up and they each took a card from a shuffled deck, returned it to the deck, and in turn each shuffled the deck. Michael then said: "Under these circumstances it would be very difficult to find your cards, wouldn't it?" All three assented. "In that case," replied Michael, "I won't even bother trying!" [Later, of course, he found the cards.]

At the same gathering, Doug Hofstadter and I had great fun acting out a skit I wrote about Martin Gardner inspired by a curious writing of his concerning Conan Doyle. This skit was later published in *The Mathemagician and Pied Puzzler*, edited by Elwyn Berlekamp and Tom Rodgers, A.K. Peters Ltd., 1999, pp. 13-17. With A.K. Peter's kind permission, here is the skit:

Martin Gardner

Ambrose, Gardner and Doyle
SCENE I — The Year is 2050 A.D.

Professor Ambrose: Have you ever read the book *Science: Good, Bad, and Bogus* by Martin Gardner?

Professor Byrd: No; I've heard of it and of course I've heard of Martin Gardner. He was a very famous science writer of the last century. Why do you ask?

Ambrose: Because the book contains one weird chapter; it is totally unlike anything Gardner ever wrote.

Byrd: Oh?

Ambrose: The chapter is titled "The Irrelevance of Conan Doyle." He actually advances the thesis that Conan Doyle never wrote the Sherlock Holmes stories—that these stories are forgeries.

Byrd: That *is* weird! Especially from Gardner! On what does he base it?

Ambrose: On absolutely nothing! His whole argument is that no one with the brilliant, rational, scientific mind to write the Sherlock Holmes stories could possibly have spent his last twelve years in a tireless crusade against all rationality—I'm talking about his crazy involvement with spiritualism.

Byrd: To tell you the truth, this fact has often puzzled me! How could anyone with the brilliance to write the Sherlock Holmes stories ever get involved with spiritualism—and in such a crazy way?

Ambrose: You mean that *you* have doubts that Doyle wrote the Holmes stories?

Byrd: Of course not! That thought has never crossed my mind! All I said was that I find the situation *puzzling.* I guess the answer is that Doyle went senile in his later years.

Ambrose: No, no! Gardner correctly pointed out that all the available evidence shows that Doyle remained quite keen and active to the end. He also pointed out that Doyle's interest in spiritualism started much earlier in life than is generally realized. So senility is not the explanation.

Byrd: I just thought of another idea! Perhaps Doyle was planning all along to foist his spiritualism on the public and started out writing his rational Holmes stories to gain everybody's confidence. Then, when the public was convinced of his rationality, whamo!

Ambrose: That's quite a cute idea! But frankly, it's just as implausible as Gardner's idea that Doyle never wrote the Holmes stories at all.

Byrd: All right, then; how do *you* explain the mystery?

Ambrose: The explanation is so obvious that I'm amazed that anyone can fail to see it!

Byrd: Well?

Ambrose: Haven't you heard of multiple personalities? Doyle obviously had a dual personality—moreover of a serious psychotic nature! The clue to the whole thing is not *senility* but *psychosis!* Surely you know that some psychotics are absolutely brilliant in certain areas and completely deluded in others. What better explanation could you have?

Byrd: You really believe that Doyle was psychotic?

Ambrose: Of course he was!

Byrd: Just because he believed in spiritualism?

Ambrose: No, his disturbance went much deeper. Don't you know that he believed that the famous Harry Houdini escaped from locked trunks by dematerializing and going out through the keyhole? What's even worse, he absolutely refused to believe Houdini when told there was a perfectly naturalistic explanation for his escapes. *He insisted that Houdini was lying!* If that's not psychotic paranoia, what is?

Byrd: I guess you're right! As I said, I never had the slightest doubt that Doyle did write the Holmes stories, but now your explanation of the apparent contradiction between Doyle the rationalist and Doyle the crank makes some sense.

Ambrose: I'm glad you realize that.

Byrd: But now something else puzzles me. Martin Gardner was no fool; he was surely one of the most interesting writers of the last century. Now, how could one of Gardner's calibre ever entertain the silly notion that Doyle never wrote the Holmes stories?

Ambrose: To me the solution is obvious: *Martin Gardner never wrote that chapter!* The chapter is a complete forgery. I have no idea *who* wrote it, but it was certainly not Martin Gardner. A person of Gardner's calibre could never have written anything like that!

Byrd: Now just a minute; are you talking about the whole book or just that one chapter?

Ambrose: Just that one chapter. All the other chapters are obviously genuine; they are perfectly consistent in spirit with all the sensible things that Gardner ever wrote. But that one chapter sticks out like a sore thumb—not just with respect to the other chapters, but in relation to all of Gardner's writings. I don't see how there can be the slightest doubt that this chapter is a complete forgery!

Byrd: But that raises serious problems! All right, I can see how an entire book by an alleged author might be a forgery, but an *isolated* chapter of a book? How could the chapter have ever gotten there? Could Gardner have hired someone to have written it? That seems ridiculous! Why would he have done a thing like that? On the other hand, why would Gardner have ever allowed the chapter to be included? Or could it possibly have gotten there without his knowledge? That also seems implausible. Will you please explain one thing: *How did the chapter ever get there?* No, your theory strikes me as most improbable!

Ambrose: I agree with you wholeheartedly; the theory *is* most improbable. But the alternative that Gardner actually wrote that chapter is not just improbable, but completely out of the question; he couldn't *possibly* have written such a chapter. And as Holmes wisely said: Whenever we have eliminated the impossible, whatever remains, *however improbable,* must be the truth. And so I am forced to the conclusion that Martin Gardner never wrote that chapter. Now, I don't go as far as some historians who believe that Martin Gardner never existed. No, I believe that he did exist, but he certainly never wrote that chapter. We can only hope that future research will answer the question of how that strange chapter ever got into the book. But surely, nobody in his right mind could believe that Gardner actually wrote that chapter.

Byrd (after a long pause): I guess you're right. In fact, the more I think about it, you *must* be right! It is certainly not conceivable that anyone as rational as Gardner could entertain such a strange notion. But now I think you've made a very important historical discovery! Why don't you publish it?

Ambrose: I am publishing it. It will appear in the June issue of the *Journal of the History of Science and Literature.* The title is *Gardner and Doyle.* I'll send you a copy.

SCENE II — One Hundred Years Later

Professor Broad: Did you get my paper, *Ambrose, Gardner and Doyle?*
Professor Cranby: No; where did you send it?

Broad: To your Connecticut address.

Cranby: Oh; then I won't get it for a couple of days. What is it about?

Broad: Well, are you familiar with the Ambrose paper, *Gardner and Doyle?*

Cranby: No; I'm familiar with much of Ambrose's excellent work, but not this one. What is it about?

Broad: You know the twentieth century writer, Martin Gardner?

Cranby: Of course! I'm quite a fan of his. I think I have just about everything he ever wrote. Why do you ask?

Broad: Well, you remember his book: *Science, Bad, and Bogus?*

Cranby: Oh, certainly.

Broad: And do you recall the chapter: "The Irrelevance of Conan Doyle?"

Cranby: Oh yes! As a matter of fact that is the strangest chapter of the book and is quite unlike anything else Gardner ever wrote. He seriously maintained that Conan Doyle never wrote the Sherlock Holmes stories.

Broad: Do *you* believe that Doyle wrote the Holmes stories?

Cranby: Of course! Why should I doubt it for one minute?

Broad: Then how do you answer Gardner's objection that no one with a mind so rational as to write the Holmes stories could possible be so irrational as to get invovled with spiritualism in the peculiarly antirational way that he did?

Cranby: Oh, come on now! That's no objection! It's obvious that Doyle, with all his brilliance, had an insane streak which simply got worse through the years. Of course, Doyle wrote the Sherlock Holmes stories!

Broad: I heartily agree!

Cranby: The one thing that puzzles me, and I remember it puzzled me at the time, is how one like Martin Gardner could ever have believed such an oddball thing!

Broad: Ah; that's the whole point of Ambrose's paper! His answer is simply that Gardner never wrote that chapter—the chapter is just a forgery.

Cranby: Good God! That's ridiculous! That's just as crazy as Gardner's idea that Doyle didn't write Holmes. Of course Gardner really wrote that chapter!

Broad: Of course he did!

Cranby: But what puzzles me is how such a sober and reliable historian as Ambrose could ever believe that Gardner didn't write that chapter. How could he ever believe anything that bizarre?

Broad: Ah; that's where *my* paper comes in! I maintain that Ambrose never wrote that paper—it must be a complete forgery!

SCENE III— A Hundred Years Later
(To be supplied by the reader)

Discussion: How come that the same Martin Gardner, so well known and highly respected for his mathematical games column which he wrote for years for the *Scientific American,* his numerous puzzle books, his annotated editions of *Alice in Wonderland, The Hunting of the Snark, The Ancient Mariner,* and *Casey at the Bat*—not to speak of his religious novel, *The Flight of Peter Fromm,* and his *Whys of a Philosophical Scrivener*—how come that he wrote such a crazy chapter as "The Irrelevance of Conan Doyle?" This troubled me for a long time, until Martin kindly informed me that the whole thing was simply a hoax!

Martin is really great on hoaxes. For example, in his April 1975 column in *Scientific American,* he reported the discovery of: a map that required five colors; an opening move in chess (pawn to Queen's Rook four) that guaranteed a certain win for White; a discovery of a fatal flaw in the theory of relativity; and a lost manuscript that proved that Leonardo da Vinci was the inventor of the flush toilet.

In Martin's book, *Whys and Wherefores* (University of Chicago Press, 1989), is reprinted a scathing review of his *The Whys of a Philosophical Scrivener* by a write named *George Groth.* The review ends with the sentence: "George Groth, by the way, is one of Gardner's pseudonyms."

• • •

Coming back to Indiana University, I stayed there for many years. I taught freshmen undergraduates and graduate students. My freshman course was an introduction to logic which started with logic puzzles and then went on to propositional logic, first-order logic and then topics in infinity. Curiously enough, many of the students were nursing students!

One incident of this course is particularly memorable. I gave a final exam with four questions. To give those students with poor mathematical ability a chance to pull up their grades, the fourth question was: "Write on any topic you like." One student wrote a story so clever that had he been an F student, I would have given him an A+, although in fact, he was an A+ student. Here is the story he wrote (as clearly as I can remember it):

> *Once upon a time, there were two tribes—the Selfish Tribe and the Altruistic Tribe. The altruists never wanted to do anything for themselves; they wanted only to do things for society. The members of the Selfish Tribe not only didn't want to do anything for society, they had a positive aversion to doing anything for society. Well, these two tribes went to war and all the people were killed except for one person from each side. The two survivors faced each other with pointed guns and were about to kill each other, when they had the following thoughts: The one from the Altruistic Tribe thought, "If I kill him, I will be the whole society and anything I do for society will really be for myself, and I don't want to be selfish." The one from the Selfish Tribe thought, "If I kill him, I'll be the whole society, hence anything I do for myself, I'll be doing for society, and I don't want to do anything for society!" And so, as a result, they didn't shoot each other.*

What do you think of that story? I think it's terrific! In a very subtle way, it actually incorporated several things he had learned in my course. Unfortunately, I lost the paper and for the life of me, I can't remember the name of the student who wrote it. If he ever reads this, I hope he will get in touch with me so that I can acknowledge his authorship.

• • •

A graduate student, one of my assistants in my course, told me the following logical joke: A man's house was burglarized, and he called his insurance agent who asked him what kind of policy he had. The man said that the policy was for fire and theft. The agent replied, "You have the wrong policy! You should have had one for fire *or* theft!"

This student also fooled me with the following two problems:

(1) In a certain small town, thirteen percent of the inhabitants had unlisted telephone numbers, and no inhabitant had more than one phone. A statistician once came into town and picked thirteen hundred names *completely at random* from the telephone book. Roughly, how many of them would you expect to have unlisted phone numbers?

(2) A certain boat had a metal ladder hanging over the side with six rungs spaced one foot apart. At low tide, the water came up to the second rung from the bottom. Then the water rose two feet. Which rung did it then hit?

I answered both questions wrongly! What are your answers? [Puzzles #31 and #32.]

Graduate Schools

In general, my graduate classes were quite interesting. I recall that in one of them, a student came in late and asked me if I could give her the notes. I replied that I would give them to her if she were good. She, being a very bright girl, asked me what it meant to be good. I replied: "It means not knowing what it means to be good." [The class loved that!]. Towards the end of my stay, a scholarship in my name was inaugurated for outstanding students, in which each year, one student wins the *Smullyan prize*.

I have had many interesting graduate students, both at Indiana and elsewhere. One remarkable student, Raymundo Morado, from Mexico, is about the most cultured person I have ever met! Besides being brilliant in mathematics, philosophy and computer science, his knowledge of history and literature was fabulous. For example, by himself he learned Italian so he could read Dante in the original! He stayed as a guest in our house in the Catskills for a week. After three days he said to me, "I don't feel as if I am a guest here; I feel as if I am living here."

One other occasion he, Blanche and I were having lunch in a restaurant. At one point he said, "You know Professor Smullyan, I really envy you!" Surprised, I asked, "Why?" He replied, "Your intelligence, wit, charm, but especially, Blanche!" A true gallant Latin gentleman!

Once I was having dinner with him and several others including one Frenchman. I couldn't resist kidding Raymundo and saying, "You know Spanish is nothing more than misspelled French." He replied, "No, no, Spanish is misspelled Latin."

Raymundo didn't write his Ph.D. thesis with me; he wrote it with Michael Dunn, who was more knowledgeable in Raymundo's sphere of interest.

Speaking of Ph.D. theses, I must tell you an amusing incident. Years ago, long before I was married, I was staying with Marvin and Gloria Minsky. One day a charming couple was visiting Marvin and the husband was having trouble writing a doctoral thesis. In my typically mischievous fashion I said to him, "I'll tell you what. I'll trade you a thesis for your wife!" Upon which Marvin interjected, "You may not know it Raymond, but she is planning to later trade *you* in for her thesis!"

I had some interesting Ph.D. students. Of course Melvin Fit-

Robert Cowen

ting was amongst them, and so were Robert Cowen, who is now a successful research mathematician teaching at Queen's College, Sue Toledo, then Sue Walker, who wrote an excellent dissertation that was subsequently published, and Malgosia Askanas, from Poland, who formalized an interesting result of the logician Alfred Tarski. Some time in the seventies, Malgosia took a graduate course with me on axiomatic set theory. At the end

Sue Walker Toledo

of the course I was supposed to give her an examination. it was in the spring and she had just rented a house for the summer with several other Polish students—a house very near our house in the Catskills. I gave her examination on an open balcony. It went as follows:—"What is your favorite theorem of this course?" She told me what it was and then I asked, "Do you know the proof?" She replied, "Yes." So I gave her an A.

Well this may shock some pedantic idiot professors, but the fact is that I knew perfectly well that she knew perfectly well what she knew and what she didn't. Many students simply don't know what they know and what they don't know, but I knew Malgosia well enough to know exactly what she knew and didn't know. Nor was my judgment faulty. As I already said, she later wrote an excellent Ph.D. dissertation.

Towards the end of my teaching days at Indiana University, Malgosia and a boyfriend of hers visited us. They sat in on the last day of a course in set theory I was giving. After everyone was seated I said to the students: "Dr. Askanas (here) took this very course with me twenty years ago. However, there is one theorem I never proved in that course, which I will prove today. If you feel that she understands the proof, I will let her keep her Ph.D., otherwise I will take it away. I'll let you all vote on it."

The students had a really great time! From Malgosia's remarks it was obvious that she understood it perfectly, and so the students voted unanimously that she keep her degree.

Music

One marvelous thing about Indiana University at Bloomington is the music department. It is as good as any music department anywhere in the world, certainly comparable to Juilliard or Curtis. Many of the students are better than many of the faculty! There are nearly a thousand student concerts a year, and my wife often attended several in one day. The now famous Joshua Bell was trained there, and my wife and I heard him when he was a child. In Bloomington, I also renewed my acquaintance with Marion Hall, an excellent pianist who was a professor in the music department

Blanche and Malgosia Askanas playing piano, four hands.

and formerly taught me for a while in Chicago.

I have already said that the reason I did not have a full concert career was the tendonitis which I still have in my right arm. This affliction has not prevented me from giving occasional concerts. A particularly interesting concert was at Rockefeller University, in which the principal item of my program was the Schubert posthumous *A Major Sonata*. I was fortunate in that two world-famous pianists, Alicia de Larrocha and Richard Goode were kind enough to listen to my program before the concert and gave me many helpful suggestions. Richard himself came to the concert [and, I am proud to say, told me it was "beautiful."]

• • •

I said earlier how I used logic to win my dear wife Blanche. She was born in Belgium of a French mother and a Dutch father. She learned both languages in her grade school days. Next to English, French is the language she knows best. Indeed, I was amused when shortly after our marriage, I was expecting a phone call one morning, and when the phone rang, Blanche sleepily said: "Raymond, it's for toi!" Curiously enough, when she counts, she still counts in Dutch.

Blanche's musical ability was manifest at a very early age. During World War I, the Germans occupied Belgium and homes were forced to house German soldiers. A German officer was housed with Blanche's family. Fortunately, he was quite musical and loved

Blanche's playing. Near the end of the war, the officer spent his furlough in Germany. When he returned, he presented Blanche with a beautiful edition of the Beethoven piano sonatas.

Blanche's older brother Henry was also quite talented. He could improvise very well on the piano, but loved jazz. He was extremely skilled in drawing and was jailed by the Germans for drawing caricatures of German soldiers on buildings.

The story of Blanche's younger brother Joseph is quite remarkable! As a child, he was very shy, quiet and often cried silently to himself. He was often laughed at and regarded as a dullard. Nobody seemed to realize his musical genius. Without any piano lessons, he would perfectly play by ear pieces he heard Blanche play, and nobody around seemed particularly impressed.

Blanche and Joseph slept upstairs in bedrooms facing each other. Both were afraid of the dark, but wouldn't come downstairs, because the few times they had, they were severely punished. To console themselves, they would sing Bach two-part inventions, Blanche singing the upper voice and Joseph perfectly singing the lower voice.

The family house faced a neighboring house and during Joseph's teenage years he would often see through the window, his neighbor, a sixteen-year-old girl with beautiful long hair, beautifully playing the violin, which Joseph could distinctly hear. At that point, Joseph decided to learn the violin, and without telling anybody, sold the bonds he had been given on previous birthdays and bought a violin. [Yes, he was quite able to do this all on his own!] He then went to the girl and asked whether she would teach him, and she agreed. For the first few days, a scratching sound came from the attic, much to the amusement of the maids who asked each other, "What on earth is that boy doing?" However, after just six months of studying, the girl told him that she had nothing more to teach him and sent him to her teacher at the conservatory. Within a year Joseph was chosen to play the Mendelssohn Violin Concerto with the orchestra. He has now been a professor of violin at the Ghent Music Conservatory for many years.

Blanche left Belgium in her late teens and went to Canada where she earned a living playing both solo and with chamber groups for various organizations. Several years later she left Canada and came to New York City teaching in a settlement school in Chatham Square funded by David Sarnoff and sponsored by Toscanini. Blanche's little boy, Jack, studied there with the now famous cellist Leonard Rose. We have a photograph of little Jack playing the cello in a Hayden trio with a violinist and the now famous Byron Janis at the piano. Byron's legs were so short then they could hardly reach the pedals! Toscanini was present and heard that performance.

Some time later, Blanche founded the *Music House* on West 88th Street—a music school where many instruments were taught, as well as theory. The faculty was excellent and included the flutist Samuel Baroon, and the cellists Leonard Rose, and Bernard Greenhouse. The eminent pianists, Ursala Oppens and Lillian Kallir were students there. Ursala was an earlier student of Blanche.

Shortly before our marriage in 1959, her former boyfriend said to her, "You're not going to marry that crazy

John Gilbert and the other musician.

guy, are you? Fortunately for that crazy guy, she married him. The two of us currently reside in New York State in the beautiful Catskill Mountains. Now, in my 83rd year, although I still write, I have returned to music as my main activity. About a year ago, a friend of mine, John Gilbert, who operates a recording studio in California, urged me to make a recording, the taping of which I have just about completed.

I play music of Bach, Scarlatti and Schubert. I have recorded my music with home materials by converting one room into a recording studio, using my wife's excellent Steinway piano, an MPA pre-amplifier and a Sony DAT recorder. Curiously enough, I got the best audio results by putting microphones *under* the piano! John Gilbert is currently in the process of engineering the tapes and converting them to CD's. How my CD fares remains to be seen. My wife's advice has been most helpful in the preparation of my recording.

• • •

I just received good news! Some time ago, the film makers, Tao and Francesco Ruspoli made a 25-minute documentary of me. A good deal of it is devoted to my music. The film has just been accepted by the International Film Festival.

• • •

Oh, one other thing; my heartfelt thanks go to the publisher Bob Long for his fantastically efficient and hard-working job of personally editing my manuscript, which I wrote at his invitation and encouragement. I also wish to add Bob Long's entire staff has been most helpful and cooperative.

That's about as much as I can say now. If new interesting events occur in my life, I will probably write them up. Let me thank you all for your kind attention.

Raymond Smullyan
Elka Park, New York
May 2002

P. S. I forget to tell you that in my childhood days I knew a man who had great grandchildren, yet none of his grandchildren had any children! How is this to be explained? [**Bonus Puzzle**]

Part III

Anatol Holt

In Chicago I came home one evening to International House and I heard someone downstairs playing the piano (Bach or Schubert). Being very attracted I listened for quite a while and, at the end, introduced myself... to Raymond Smullyan who had decided to play the grand piano in the "living room" of International house.

As of that evening, I became very involved with Raymond. At that time he was teaching piano at Roosevelt College in Chicago, but already had a lot of pain in his arms because of tendonitis; because of this he was seriously thinking of giving up a career as a concert pianist. As far as I knew, Raymond had no formal education, but, without question, was a genius... and that in three fields: music, magic, and mathematics.

Soon he moved from Roosevelt College to a nightclub, where he did stupefying tricks to the delight of the nightly audience.

Many years later Raymond was "discovered" by a mathematics professor at Princeton. This professor extracted Raymond from his Chicago nightclub, gave him a Ph.D. in mathematics, and installed him as a professor of logic at Princeton University.

Nine months after I met him, I got together with him in New York where, every night from midnight on, he taught me Galois Theory. It was the first time that I understood that MATH-EMATICS COULD BE BEAUTIFUL — something which I had not learned in my previous mathematical education, and something which played an important role in my life years later when I chose to concentrate on mathematics at Harvard.

One more, vaguely related Raymond story of my personal experience. Circa 1955, he came to visit me in Philadelphia. "Well, Tolly... what are you doing now?" he inquired. I told him about my job as computer programmer with John Mauchly and UNIVAC I (at Remington Rand). "A *computer* you say? What's that?" I began an explanation. Five minutes later, Raymond, a little bewildered and with a very wrinkled forehead, stopped me: "Tolly... explain to me what a computer is, in words that any mathematician would understand. "Well...," I tried again; Raymond did not interrupt me this time; his consternation had transformed into "cloudy skies."

I will not chronicle Raymond's public career in the many years that have passed since, except to say: he has published many books and papers, often whimsical *and* profound. Some critics have called him the Lewis Carroll of our day.

My attraction to Raymond was based, first and foremost, on music and secondly on mathematics (me never having been interested in magic). But, I have always been an aesthete!! And it is that, above all, which united me to Raymond's music and mathematics.

I was always fascinated by Raymond's superb aesthetiic sense and his basic honesty, and remain so till the present day.

The Tao is Silent

This is a book by Raymond that I ran into titled *The Tao is Silent* (New York City, Harper & Row Publishers, 1977). No, I haven't finished reading it, but I feel moved to tell you about my experience with it so far.

Early on in the book, Raymond asks (rhetorically): does the Tao *exist*, just as, in the West, people have (seriously) asked (and argued about) whether God exists. Perhaps these questions seem serious and philosophical to you; no doubt they are, but I also think of them a little with (Smullyanesque) whimsy.

In an early chapter he raises yet another, analogous question of existence: do *melodies* exist? He means, "melodies" as distinct from an aggregate of pitches, for, as he observes: there are plenty of people who perceive aggregates of pitches, while (apparently) not hearing melodies. I agree with Smullyan: the Tao is a particularly interesting "something," since its adepts consider it is as much "nothing" as "something," and furthermore consider that no thing could *be* (or not be) without it, (not even itself). Having once *seen* It, you can never again be alone or abandoned; (never experience the despair of Jesus on the cross who cried, "Eli, Eli, lama shabachtani?").

To feel alone and abandoned *is* the worst fate that can befall a human being. For most people, only the context of me-and-my-kind can possibly sustain the sense of existence—of *anything,* even of yourself; but for an adept of the Tao, *no* evidence of abandoment by "his kind" can cast him into despair. (Perhaps this is what "salvation" *does* mean, or *might* mean!)

This discourse naturally leads to "purpose," so fundamental to our consciousness (and so despised by Science). Once, having been asked about the "purpose of life," I replied, "Life doesn't *have* a purpose; Life is the source of purposes."

Story after story in Raymond's book illustrates the Tao adepts freedom from purpose. This relates to three positive aspects of his life: it opens his heart, his eye, and his mind, for *purpose* constrains all three—it inures him against failure and disappointments, it contributes powerfully to his creativity.

Anatol Holt

Douglas R. Hofstadter

M y first encounter with Raymond Smullyan was in roughly 1961, when as a high-school student fascinated by mathematical logic and Gödel's *Incompleteness Theorem*, I ran into his concise technical monograph *Theory of Formal Systems*. This book had a fantastically beautiful way of showing how all the mathematical properties of numbers (e.g., the primeness of 89) come out of the way they are represented in symbols (e.g., the juxtaposition of the digits "8" and "9", or the sequence "122121" representing 89 in dyadic notation). It revealed in a dazzlingly clear manner the non-obvious but profoundly important fact that in mathematics, semantics—the set of truths about the world—emerges from syntax—the rules that govern symbols. I was so fascinated by this revelation that for months I played around with the kinds of formal systems that Smullyan had shown. From Smullyan's little book I also learned new and extraordinarily clear ways of visualizing the "twisting-back" of self-reference that lies at the core of Gödel's proof. All of this experience deeply enriched me, became a permanent part of me, and many years later reemerged, in a new form, in my own book *Gödel, Escher, Bach: an Eternal Golden Braid*, in which, in my bibliography, I indicated my profound indebtedness to Raymond Smullyan.

My next encounter with Smullyan was in 1980 or so, when I was visiting the home of Martin Gardner (of *Mathematical Games* fame), to discuss the extremely interesting but also extremely daunting idea that I might take over his slot in *Scientific American* magazine. Martin and I were in his study discussing something when the phone rang, and it turned out to be none other than Raymond Smullyan, telling Martin about a book that he had just written, entitled *The Tao is Silent*. The idea that a highly technical logician would write a book on Taoism struck me as fascinating, and when I got a copy I was instantly absorbed by his engaging, often hilarious style and his amazingly fresh way of looking at things. I didn't myself buy into the Taoistic philosophy, but I found Smullyan's writing on it so rich and so filled with extraordinarily thought-provoking comments that I read it and reread it with enormous interest. Just as Smullyan's ideas about logic had enriched my first book, so these ideas about mind and soul and related issues enriched the next book that I worked on, which was *The Mind's I,* coedited with philosopher Daniel Dennett. In that book, we used a marvelously witty and stimulating dialogue called "Is God a Taoist?" from *The Tao is Silent,* and also two other pieces by Ray that appeared in subsequent books of his philosophical musings.

And then, of all things, it turned out that Smullyan was coming to join the Philosophy Department of Indiana University, where I worked. It was a strange twist of fate.

I remember meeting Ray at a party at which he went up to various women there and said to them, "Bet you a nickel I can kiss you without touching you!," and then, quite predictably, he would kiss their faces and say, with a broad smile say, "Gee, I lose!" He also gleefully performed numerous magic tricks, usually with small objects, at these parties, and did so with great dexterity.

One of Ray's greatest skills is in misleading the eye, as in his magic tricks, or misleading the mind, as in his magical books on chess puzzles—*The Chess Mysteries of Sherlock Holmes* and *The Chess Mysteries of the Arabian Knights.* Typical of what Ray does in the former is he has Holmes and Watson discussing a chess board that they come across in a chess club, and Watson speculates about how it could have come to be in the state it is in, and I, as a reader, follow Watson's reasoning very clearly, and it seems absolutely perfect and flawless. I am convinced 100% of what Watson has said. And then, devastatingly, Raymond has Holmes come out with a total refutation of Watson's analysis. Watson has forgotten some obscure possibility, but one that was perfectly available for anyone (e.g., me) to see. It makes me, as a reader who feels somewhat proud of his mind and his ability to think clearly, rather ashamed and also a bit worried about my own ability to analyze situations. And then sometimes, even more confusingly, Raymond will do this same thing twice over. There may be someone else who first refutes Watson, revealing something crucial that Watson (and of course I too) missed, again to be refuted by Holmes—or perhaps it is Holmes himself who self-corrects in the end. But always there is a twist where one (that is to say, me) falls for what seems like perfect, flawless reasoning, and then one has one's total comeuppance. It is exceedingly disorienting, perhaps even discouraging at times, just as is a magic trick for which one can imagine no reasonable explanation. One loses confidence in one's own mind!

Well, this kind of virtuosic and delightful intellectual trickery gives rise to many ponderings, naturally. One day, I heard Ray deliver a magnificent lecture, at Indiana University, on the convoluted reasoning that goes into Gödel's famous *Second Theorem* (about the impossibility of a formal system containing a proof of its own consistency). Ray was showing us how to think about this issue via some beautiful analogies he had developed over the years, and the reasoning, though clear, was exceedingly tricky. I kept on feeling that I wasn't nearly as sure of my footing as the old mountain goat up on stage was. He just kept on saying that one thing followed necessarily from another, and I kept on wondering why, and finally, when he had finished, I timidly raised my hand and, when he called on me, I came out with a rather long monologue.

"Ray," I said, "I am a bit puzzled. You are working in a domain that is absolutely filled with dangerous pitfalls—places where the mind can so easily fall into traps. And yet you are telling us with such total, serene confidence that the reasoning pathway that you are showing us has fallen into no traps, has overlooked no alternatives, and so forth. But in your magnificent books on chess puzzles, you give us shining examples of someone who does just that—Dr. Watson—and then you always have Watson's perfectly convincing reasoning refuted in a devastating manner by someone of greater insight. How, then, can I, as a listener to your talk, be sure that you are not just deliberately pulling the wool over our eyes? Perhaps you are going to have a second lecture on this same topic next week, and in that lecture you will reveal to us that what you showed us THIS week was in fact totally confused and wrong. One week from today, you are going to show us that today you were playing the 'Watson' role. You are going to be Sherlock Holmes next week, and make us feel ashamed for falling lock, stock, and barrel for the sloppy reasoning of this week—even though this week it looks totally flawless. Do you see what I mean, Ray?"

Raymond beamed at me with delight and was about to reply, when I said, "Before you answer, please let me go on with my musing for just a moment more, all right? Because I have an even more worrisome issue to raise. Perhaps you are not, in fact, deliberately playing the Dr. Watson role this week. Perhaps, in fact, you are convinced that you have given us the final flawless Holmesian analysis of this situation. But look. Already a little 8x8 chessboard is, as you have so masterfully shown us in your puzzle books, a field filled with hidden mines all over the place. Even in this tiny, concrete, finite universe of chess positions, it is so easy for a relatively good thinker like me to be totally misled by what seems like ironclad reasoning. That's what you've masterfully taught me, Raymond Smullyan. All right, then—what about mathematical logic, which is a far more abstract and infinite domain? If Sherlock Holmes can one-up Dr. Watson in chess, then who's to say that someone couldn't play Holmes to YOU, Ray? Maybe YOU have missed something here, just as your Watson character was always missing something on the chessboard, despite at first sight seeming to have seen everything. Why couldn't some Supersmullyan character step out of the wings and say, 'Okay, folks, Professor Smullyan here has just given you some convincing and very subtle arguments to convince you about Gödel's *Second Theorem*—but now I am going to show you where there lies a subtle flaw in what he said. Professor Smullyan's reasoning is riddled with subtle holes, in truth...' What do you say to this scenario, Ray? Don't you ever pause to ask yourself if, despite your own deep convictions of seeing everything here, you aren't somehow missing or overlooking some exceedingly subtle fatal error? Or to put it more bluntly, even if YOU are not worried about this scenario, you have been so clever in your chess-puzzle books as to instill doubt in my mind about ANY subtle reasoning procedure, including even those of Sherlock Holmes, including even those of Raymond Smullyan himself, and even of the hypothetical Supersmullyan who might one-up you..."

I was not being tongue-in-cheek whatsoever in my questions and my musings. Unfortunately, I don't recall how Ray replied to this long-winded monologue, but I do know that I still feel worried in exactly the way I expressed myself that day.

Ray has since come out with a several puzzle books and a couple of highly technical books that take some of the ideas in this marvelous lecture and expound them in print. One of his enormous gifts is to take these difficult and very abstract ideas and to turn them into hilarious episodes in fictitious worlds inhabited by crazy truth-telling knights and always-lying knaves, and other much weirder characters. One gets the feeling, though, at times, that one has seen these basic themes before, even if each new setting is fresh and engaging. It's as if Ray were a composer of music who writes a magnificent set of variations on a theme, and you love them all—and then he comes out with another magnificent set of variations on another theme, and then another and another—and after a while, you notice that oddly enough, the themes on which each new set is based are themselves all variations on a deeper theme! In other words, Ray's themes themselves are variations on a very deep theme. Is that possible? I will come back to that thought at the end of my recollections.

Raymond has an extremely playful soul and he loves thinking about games of all sorts. He got deeply involved in thinking about the philosophical issues raised by the Prisoner's Dilemma, when I wrote about it in one of my *Scientific American* columns, and I recall the intensity with which we debated the issues over lunch one day.

And then one day we were invited to a student dormitory to have a debate about soul and mind, a topic about which I knew we disagreed, and I proposed to Ray that, just for fun, we exchange roles. I wanted to see if he could really give voice to my position (which was expounded in *The Mind's I*, and which of course he had read)—I wanted to see if he had internalized it clearly

Hofstadter, student, me.

or not. Well, Ray loved the idea of this role-swapping, and as soon as he opened his mouth in our reversed-roles debate, he came out with the hilarious remark, presumably addressed to himself by me, "What do YOU know about these things, you hairy old mystic?'" I cracked up. And I have to admit that he was excellent at mouthing my own positions, whereas I felt completely tongue-tied, trying to explain his positions. So much for my great idea of swapping roles.

Raymond has always been a most generous person, kind and concerned, and it has been a particular pleasure to see him in the company of Blanche, his wife, another grand human being. I will always recall a fascinating conversation I had with Blanche about the difference between their musical interests. Both of them are excellent pianists, but Raymond is very happy to perform in front of people all the time, whereas Blanche is far more reticent. I noticed, after Ray had come to several parties at my house and played piano at them all, that he always played exactly the same set of pieces—very impressively and also very expressively. I mentioned this curious fact to Blanche, and she said,

"Yes, I know—this is Ray's style all over. I am the diametric opposite. I will work very hard for weeks or months on a piece in order to master it, but then I will leave it and go on to another. And I am never satisfied with what I have mastered. I need continual novelty. Raymond is the opposite. He is deeply in love with what he has. He can play it over and over again without ever tiring of it. He is faithful to it, and he simply savors it repeatedly in the most innocent manner possible. I wish I had that gift, but I do not."

I believe that in these words about Ray's style, Blanche hit on something deep at the core of her husband. Ray loves one thing, but that one thing is so deep and so complex that he finds a million ways of exploiting it and always giving us new perspectives and views on it. Raymond Smullyan has enriched us all in his extreme determination to keep on grappling forever with the one marvelous hidden theme that lies at the very core of his being.

Douglas R. Hofstadter
College of Arts and Sciences
Professor of Cognitive Science
Indiana University, Bloomington

Robert Cowen

I first met Ray while I was an undergraduate at Princeton in 1958. I took the logic course offered by the math department (I was a math major) and fortunately, it turned out, Professor Alonzo Church was on leave and Ray Smullyan, his Ph.D student, was filling in for Church (which also meant he had the use of Church's very nice office). The course he gave was like no other course I had taken. He was perfecting his tableau method for doing logical proofs and it was really exciting. He would do something one way and then the next day he would find a better way or explanation. Mathematics was being created right before our eyes! But of course that is the way Ray always teaches, as I later found out. We had something else in common also.

He became interested in astronomy and sought my advice when I told him that I had constructed my own reflecting telescope.

Largely because of his course, I decided to study logic in graduate school. I went to Cornell because the logician Barkley Rosser was there but wasn't happy at Cornell. I had ceased being excited about mathematics. Meanwhile Ray went to Yeshiva, joining Martin Davis in a new graduate program (which also had attracted to their faculty Donald Newman and Louis Auslander). So after obtaining an MA from Cornell, I moved back home to New York City and enrolled in Yeshiva. The atmosphere was wonderfully warm and friendly. I took Ray's set theory course and of course he was writing his own notes, that is, each week a student 'volunteer' would write up the lectures and distribute them. Again I felt excited about mathematics. He later published a book based on this course with Mel Fitting, who also was a student at Yeshiva. I did my Ph.D. thesis on set theory under Ray and got a job at Queens College where I have remained to this day.

I kept up with Ray and his wife Blanche, visiting them in their new home in Tannersville with my wife Ilsa, and my daughters, Lenore and Minda. Ray was a wonderful host for children of all ages! He would tell fabulous stories and outrageous jokes. He would do magic tricks—pull coins out of your ears and then fool you again and again with clever card tricks and puzzles. And what puzzles they were! When Ray was working on his first puzzle book, *What is the Name of this Book?*, he sent me a draft to proof-read. I gave it to Lenore who was then a rather precocious ten-year-old. She was enthralled. She read it very carefully and even made some corrections. She later confided to me that her opinion of me went way up because I was a student of Raymond Smullyan. She felt that by getting to know Ray and reading the book, she was being admitted into a wonderful club and it was all 'very cool.' I am convinced that this experience had a lot to do with her becoming a mathematician.

Ray gave a talk recently in honor of Mel Fitting's 60th birthday called "Logical Legerdemain" and I was glad to see that he hasn't changed at all. Still doing magic tricks, puzzles and fooling people with boyish delight! The point, as always, was ultimately serious and the puzzles, of course, are deeply profound. As I left, I saw two graduate students attending with their baby. I recommended they get Ray's book for their child as soon as possible!

Gloria and Marvin Minsky

Raymond Smullyan was the best of my teen-aged cousins, or the better, as I had only one other that I knew at the time of my childhood, and he was a sports buff.

My first memory of Raymond was on a summer day at my parents (all year round) beach house. I was sitting at a square table on the front porch enjoying an ocean breeze and "chomping at the bit" waiting for our "dear relatives"—in my mind, either from England or New York City. I'd met Raymond's parents and they spoke with a British accent. To wait for a teen-aged "skadey-eighth" (3rd or 4th) cousin seemed the height of punishment for a young kid. So up comes a gangly boy, says hello, hands me a penny and asks "What would be your first move that would guarantee winning if you went first and I went second on this (square) table? A guardian angel on my shoulder (another name for a synapse that clicked) guided my little hand to place the penny in the very center of the table. That, and a few other simple puzzles apparently made up for my not playing chess or other more cerebral games, and we clicked as friends.

My next encounter with Raymond did not take place for a long time, though I continued to hear "oohs and ahs" of admiration by my parents and grandparents and "tsks" of disappointment and sympathy, because we had heard that Raymond was on the verge of expulsion at a New York high school for wearing a derby, smoking a cigar, and letting teachers know that he knew more than they did (the latter probably true). The disappointment seemed to be in the stupidity of teachers who didn't know genius when they see it and hear it.

I don't remember seeing Raymond again for a very long time, though his beautiful actress-ambitious sister and his parents visited many times, especially in the summer. In fact, in my mid-teens, as a junior in college, precociously four years ahead of my  peers, I actually *didn't want* to see Raymond. This was for two main reasons: one was that I feared being confronted with hard puzzles that I wouldn't be able to solve and therefore would look and feel dumb. The other reason involved relatives whispering about romantic possibilities (he was a "distant" cousin). I would never put up with suggested dating partners, especially anyone suggested by a family member.

I actually did see Raymond once—he was about to be in a play or a magic show and his mother had made a marvelopus cape—black on one side, red on the other, which he demonstrated with great pride and panache. Around that time I also met for the first time that I recall, Raymond's older brother Emile, also much admired by the family. He was either a full blown economist or an economist-to-be. Emile was a somewhat mysterious and remote figure to me, very nice personally, but set up as an icon and therefore not very reachable.

Next, I'm young and married and just out of medical school and visiting Chicago with my husband, Marvin Minsky. For some (good) reason we looked up Raymond who was now featured as "Five-Ace Merrill" starring at the Pump Room of some famous hotel. Raymond's sleight-of-hand magic was unwordly and marvelous. Because he was really a mathematician by day, he and Marvin (also a mathematician at that time) got along famously and much to my delight.

Marvin got together with Raymond a few times without me on trips to Chicago.

Our then dog, Senje, also made a hit with Raymond, and he

has reminded us, over the years, how Senje jumped up on a chair at one of our dinner parties and started to eat Margaret's supper only to be admonished (by Margaret), "No, Senje, that's *my* dinner!"

Raymond also did some magic tricks for our friends and their children. One eight year old boy was very sassy and Raymond "scolded" him by saying, "I eat little boys like you," to which the not-to-be-ployed little boy replied, "And I eat big men like you."

As may be imagined, we had really fun times, and always looked forward to Raymond's visits.

Then I remember in the late 50s early 60s a few Raymond visits to our house in Cambridge, Mass. When our first child (Margaret) was about two or three. Raymond had a wonderful way with little kids (to whom magic is an extension, not a replacement for the real world). He had an inexhaustible supply of games, puzzles, and questions. In other words he was a complete "hit" with Margaret, who luckily was able to hold her own with Raymond.

Raymond visited us a few times when we lived in an apartment on Newbury St. in Boston (pre-children). On one of his visits he left behind one of his "how-to" magic books. Before sending it back to him, both Marvin and I leapt into it—determined to learn magic and astound Raymond at his next visit. Alas, directions like "force a card by your favorite method and then..." put a damper on us novices who did not have access to the previous volume which told you *how* to "force a card." We continue to be astounded by Raymond's sleight of hand; truly magical.

Though we continued to be astounded by Raymond's magic as time went by it seemed that his magic feats were playing second fiddle to his mathematician/logician persona.

Over the years I found more cousins hither and yon who I did not know as a child. Raymond continues to be my favorite.

Gloria Rudisch

As a world-class close-range prestidigitator, Smullyan shows us that our senses reveal less of what there actually is than of what our minds expect us to see. And as a master of Paradox, he demonstrates how frequently commonsense thinking, too, can deceive us. We're fortunate to know such minds—but we rarely encounter a brain like this, that has managed to mix such strange physical tricks with so much grace and eloquence that one wonders whether he truly exists. (He once lived in our home for an entire year—but we're not sure that we ever saw him there.)

Also a master comedian too—he shows us the jokes in everything. Through examples from chess, language, music, and logic, Smullyan proves that our world is more comic than anyone could ever imagine.

None of this happened by accident. One might search for the source of this vast mass of talents but I doubt that this quest would meet any success, because what Raymond does appears to stem from a singular meta-dexterity, based on perceiving self-reference beneath the surface of everything. As the most recursive person there is, he neither had nor needed a cause; he simply asserted that 'I exist'—and then left the rest to consistency.

marvin minsky

Ann Close

The temptation when writing about Raymond Smullyan is to try to figure out how to be as delightful and thought-provoking as he is. But since that is impossible, I'll just settle in and try to describe the experience.

I met him first, of course, through a manuscript, *The Chess Mysteries of Sherlock Holmes,* a series of chess puzzles, all set in fitting Holmes and Watson dialogues. Each puzzle gave the reader a position on a chess board and asked him to work out the moves that could have gotten the pieces to that position. Retrograde analysis it is called. So I knew Raymond's gently insisting, questioning turn of mind before I actually met him.

As I recall, he appeared in my office, almost magically, and I mean that literally. Of course, he is a magician, and he looks it, with his entrancing beard and quizzical manner. His tendency to pull coins from your ears confirms it. In fact, he seems to move in an aura of magic, and that's one of the reasons it's always so much fun to be around him. That plus his loving, mischievous spirit as he poses mathematical and logical puzzles just for you. Or so it seems.

Such was Raymond Smullyan's magic, in fact, that it led me, who thought of myself up till then as mathematically challenged, to publish another book of chess puzzles, *The Chess Mysteries of the Arabian Knights,* and then five books of logic puzzles. These include *The Lady or the Tiger? To Mock a Mockingbird; Forever*

Undecided; Satan, Cantor and Infinity; and *The Riddle of Scheherazade.* Each book is a delight in its own way, each a combination of mind-twisting puzzles and metapuzzles, with a long "mathematical novel" that leads you in labyrinthine ways to a major mathematical concept, unsually to do with Gödel, whose incompletness theorem revolutionized mathematical thinking in the early twentieth century.

So it has been my great pleasure and luck to have known and worked with Raymond Smullyan. He has taken me to realms of mind that I never thought I could enter and, in a more earthbound way, has been a wonderful friend. In all the years we've worked together, I don't think we've ever had even a slight disagreement (although I know he didn't like several of his book jackets) or anything but the happiest of times. And I look forward to more and better times with Raymond—and maybe another book.

Ann Close

Nice Things

I once called Ann at her mother's home in South Carolina. She wasn't in but I spoke to her mother. At one point I asked, "Are you as beautiful, charming, and talented as your daughter?" She responded, "Oh, much more so!"

Mel Fitting

When I was in graduate school there were two logicians on the faculty, Smullyan, and Martin Davis. I was taking a course with Davis, and he was covering what he called "Smullyan's Theorem," a simplified version of one of the Hilbert epsilon theorems. It was difficult to hear Davis because there was a lot of loud talking in the hallway. Finally Davis had enough and called out, "Please be quiet, there's a class going on." A very abashed Smullyan stuck his head in the door and apologized, and we went on with Smullyan's theorem.

Graduate school was a division of Yeshiva University, though as a graduate school it had no particular religious aspects. There was a man who came around fairly regularly, I can't remember his name any more, who believed he was God. He passed out Xeroxed writings, mostly numerology, very densely written. Not surprisingly, his presence was objected to by the administration. Raymond, however, used to invite him into his office and talk with him. His position was, "He says he's God, can they prove he's not?"

My first wife and I were married at the Smullyan home in Elka Park. Sometime later we were visiting there, and Raymond had acquired a dog, Peekaboo. She had not been altered, was in heat, and the house was surrounded constantly by a very large number of male dogs, peering in every window. The difficulty was in arranging for Peekaboo to relieve herself. Finally the following plan was worked out. The front door was opened and all the male dogs rushed onto the porch, after which the door was closed. My wife and I handed Peekaboo out the bedroom window, she was loaded into Raymond's car, driven a safe distance, and let out. I don't think the male dogs ever figured it out.

More on the Dog Business

Mel was married in our house in Elka Park by a local Justice of the Peace. When the Justice came into the house, he had to pass through the porch, on which Peekaboo and a male dog were mating! The Justice was highly embarrassed, and Blanche, who saw this said: "Perhaps you better marry *them* first!" The poor Justice was so confused that when he came to marrying the couple he got Melvin's name all wrong and said, "Do you, Felix, take Greer to be your lawful wife?"

The couple stayed in our house a whole week after the ceremony, and on the first few nights the male dogs were outside howling all over the place! Greer regarded this as a symbol of fertility, and indeed, during that time she got pregnant with Miriam.

Leon Kirchner

Raymond and I roomed together at Berkeley, California in 1939, when I was attending the University. We once gave a joint recital there. In 1942, Raymond and I were living in New York. At that time he was undecided whether to make music or mathematics his profession. I then knew the famous pianist Mieczyslaw Horszowski and arranged for Raymond to have an audition with him. Raymond came back from the audition looking disappointed and said that Horszowski had said something to the effect that Raymond came a week too late. Well, many, many years later, when Horszowski was in his late nineties, I was having breakfast with him at the Marlboro Music Festival and somehow Raymond's name came up and I asked Horszowski whether he remembered him. He replied, "Oh yes, whatever happened to him?" I reminded him of the audition and of Raymond's disappointment at what he had said. He replied, "Oh no, he misunderstood me! What I meant was that the registration at the Curtis School of Music had occurred a week before Raymond came to me, and had he come a week earlier, I could have arranged for him to get a scholarship there to study with Rudolph Serkin." I told this to Raymond a few weeks ago, wondering whether he would feel pleased or disappointed. He was actually very pleased!

In 1957, my wife and I once visited a colleague of the Institute for Advanced Study in Princeton, NJ. At one point he told us he had to leave to go to a lecture. "In psychology?," I asked. "Oh no," he replied. "A group of us are going to a class given by a famous mathematician who is also a fabulous magician!" When I asked what was his name, he replied, "Raymond Smullyan."

Books

1. *The Tao Is Silent,* Harper and Row, 1977. Has also appeared in Japanese, Greek, Polish, German, Dutch, Russian, Korean and Hebrew.
2. *What Is the Name of this Book?*, Prentice-Hall, 1978. Has also appeared in French, Italian, Spanish, German, Dutch, Russian, Polish, Bulgarian, Hungarian, and Japanese.
3. *The Chess mysteries of Sherlock Holmes,* Alfred A. Knopf, 1979. Has also appeared in German, French, Spanish, Polish, and Yugoslavian. Will appear in Russian.
4. *This Book Needs No Title,* Prentice-Hall, 1980. Some of these essays have been reprinted in *The Mind's Eye* by Douglas Hofstadter and Daniel Dennet, Basic Books, 1981.
5. *The Chess Mysteries of the Arabian Knights,* Alfred A,. Knopf, 1982. Has also appeared in German, Spanish, and Yugoslavian. Will appear in Russian.
6. *The Lady or the Tiger?*, Alfred A. Knopf, 1982. Has also appeared in French, Italian, Spanish, German, Dutch, Danish, Russian, Yugoslavian, Hungarian, and Greek.
7. *Alice in Puzzleland,* William Morrow & Co., 1982. Has also appeared in German, Spanish, Yugoslavian, Russian, Japanese and Portuguese.
8. *5000 B. C.—And Other Philosophical Fantasies,* St. Martin's Press, 1983. Has also appeared in German, Italian, and Spanish.
9. *To Mock a Mockingbird,* Alfred A. Knopf, 1985. Has also appeared in German, Spanish, Yugoslavian, and Japanese.

10. *Forever Undecided,* Alfred A. Knopf, 1987. Has also appeared in German, Spanish, Yugoslavian, and Japanese.
11. *Satan, Cantor and Infinity,* Alfred A. Knopf, 1992. Has appeared in French, German, and Yugoslavian. Will appear in Italian, Bulgarian, and Japanese.
12. *The Riddle of Scheherazade and Other Amazing Puzzles, Ancient and Modern,* Alfred A. Knopf, 1997. As also appeared in French, Chinese, Spanish, and Portuguese.
13. *Some Interesting Memories,* Thinkers' Press.
14. *Who Knows?—A Study of Religious Consciousness,* Indiana University Press (to appear).

Submitted for Publication and Work in Progress

1. *The Magic Garden of George B.* (An introduction to Boolean Algebra.) Submitted to Alfred A. Knopf.
2. *A Children's Puzzle Book.* (In preparation)
3. *Logical Labyrinths—A Bridge From Logic Puzzles to Mathematical Logic.* (In preparation)

My favorite picture with Blanche.

Part IV

SOLUTIONS TO PUZZLES

1 - Nothing is greater than God, the dead eat nothing, and if the living eat nothing, they die. Thus, the answer is *nothing*.

This reminds me of a riddle I heard: Which is better, eternal happiness or a ham sandwich? Well, nothing is better than eternal happiness, and a ham sandwich is better than nothing. Hence, a ham sandwich is better than eternal happiness.

This is similar to the proof that every cat has ten lives: No cat has nine lives, and one cat has one more life than no cat. Therefore, a cat has ten lives.

2 - It is remarkable how many people get the wrong answer to this! They put themselves in the place of the man looking at the picture and reason: "Since I have no brothers or sister, then my father's son must be me." So far, that reasoning is correct. But then, they falsely conclude: "Therefore, I am looking at a picture of myself." This is wrong! If the man had said, "This *man* is my father's son, then he would indeed be looking at a picture of himself, but he didn't say that. He said that this man's *father* is my father's son, which is tantamount to saying that the man's father is myself, which means that he is looking at a picture of his son.

3 - It is impossible that there could exist *both* an irresistible cannonball *and* an immobile post. If a cannonball could knock over *anything* it hits, then no post could resist it, hence no post could be immovable. It is logically possible that there could be an irre-

sistible cannonball, and it is logically possible that there could be an immovable post, but it is not logically possible that there could be *both!*

4 - If Black had a certain win, White could pass in his first move and effectively become Black.

5 - How can 90 days fit between a day in January and a day in May? Consulting a calendar, we see that there are exactly 90 days between January 31 and May 1 *providing* it is not a leap year! In a leap year, the shortest possible time between any day in January and any day in May is 91 days (since February 29 falls in between). This proves that Bernard's 47th birthday cannot fall in a leap year, hence he could not have been 47 in 1980, which is 47 years after 1933. And so, Bernard couldn't have been born in 1933, hence was born in 1932 and so is older than Arthur.

6 - Call the three men *A*, *B*, and *C*, but let *C* be the clever man who knew what he had. Well, *C* realized that if he had a green stamp, then *B*, knowing that *A* saw a red stamp, would know that it was *his* red stamp that *A* saw, and so would have lowered his hand. Since *B* didn't lower his hand, then *C* realized that he couldn't have a green stamp. [Also, if *C* had had a green stamp, *A* would have also known what he had.]

7 - Let us first consider the simpler problem in which *C* saw 2 greens on *B* and 2 reds on *A*. Well, *C* realized that if he had 2 reds, *A* would have seen 4 reds and would have known that he must have 2 greens, and that if he had 2 greens, *B* would have seen 4 greens and would have known that he had 2 reds. Thus, *C* realized that he couldn't have either 2 reds or 2 greens.

Now let us consider the more difficult problem in which each one got a red and a green and *B* knew what he had on the second round. He then reasoned that if he had 2 of the same color—say 2 reds—then *A* would have known on the second round what he had, because seeing 3 reds, he would know that he couldn't have 2 reds, and also would have known that if he had two greens, C would have seen B with 2 reds and A with 2 greens and would then have known what he had (by the same reasoning of the simpler problem above.)

8 - Moses didn't have an ark; it was Noah.

9 - A statement that would work is: "I am an uncertified liar." A truth-teller would never say that, so the speaker must be a liar. Since he lied, his statement is false, which means he is not an uncertified liar. Since he is a liar, he must be a certified liar.

10 - He could have said, "I am either a certified truth-teller or an uncertified liar." If his statement is true, then he must be a certified truth-teller (since he couldn't be an uncertified liar). If his statement is false, then he is neither a certified truth-teller nor an uncertified liar, and being a liar but not an uncertified one, he must be a certified liar. Thus, there is no way of knowing whether he is truthful or not, but in either case he is certified.

11 - All he need say is: "I am certified. If he is truthful, then he really is certified and hence a certified truth-teller. If he is a liar, then he is really not certified, hence he is than an uncertified liar. There is no way of telling which.

12 - The native asserted that at least one of the following alternatives holds:
(1) He is a liar.
(2) There is gold on the island.

If he were a liar, then the first alternative would hold, hence his statement would be true, but liars do not make true statements, and so he must be truthful. Since he is truthful, then one of the two alterna-

WFIU's "Puzzle Time" with philosophy Professor Raymond Smullyan.

tives really does hold, but it cannot be (1), so it must be (2). Thence, he is a truth-teller and there is gold on the island.

13 - It cannot be determined what *Bal* means, but it can be determined whether or not he is truthful: Suppose *Bal* means *yes,* then he affirmed that *Bal* meant *yes,* and he was right. On the other hand, suppose that *Bal* means *no,* then he denied that *Bal* meant *yes,* and again he was right. And so, he is a truth-teller.

14 - All you need do is ask him if he is truthful. Both truth-tellers and liars would claim to be truthful, hence whatever word he answers must mean *yes.*

15 - He was Napoleon.

16 - I sometimes like to horse around! I told you he was lazily lying in the sun, hence he was *lying,* so his name was really Edwin. [All right! All right!]

17 - He in effect said that he has said before what he is now saying. Now, suppose he is a truth-teller. Then he really did say the same thing before. When he did, he was also truthful then too, so he must have said it at a time before that, hence also a time before that, and a time before that... and so on *ad infinitum.* Thus, unless the guy has lived infinitely far back in the past, he can't be a truth-teller.

Here is perhaps a simpler way of looking at it. Since he made that statement once, there must have been a first time that he said it, and when he said it then, it was clearly false. Thus, he is a liar.

18 - Again, there must have been a first time when he made that statement, and then it must have been true. Thus, he is a truth-teller.

19 - The argument is actually valid. Yes, it is! You see, since everyone loves my baby, then my baby being a person, loves my baby. And so, my baby loves my baby and my baby loves *only* me. Therefore, my baby and I must be the same person!

20 - This argument is also valid. Since Romeo loves Juliet, then Romeo is a lover. Hence, everyone loves Romeo. Hence, everyone is a lover. Hence everyone loves everyone! In particular Iago loves Othello.

21 - The statement I had in mind was something like: "I am a married liar. A truth-teller couldn't say that, hence he was a liar. Since he lied, then he was not really a married liar, so he was actually an unmarried liar. But I had no way of knowing that before he spoke!

In a lecture I once gave, a high-school student thought of a much cuter solution: "I am mute."

22 - It is impossible! How is that known? Perhaps a computer could examine all conceivable cases, but that would take a God-awful bit of time! However, there is the following amazingly simple and strikingly elegant proof of the impossibility.

Imagine the squares alternately colored black and red, just like a checkerboard. Now, each domino must cover one black square and one red square, hence the number of red squares covered by the dominoes would have to be the same as the number of black squares covered. This is impossible if two diagonally opposite corner squares are removed, because they are of the same color (both red, say, which would mean that there are only 30 red squares left and 32 black squares).

Incidentally, I have heard that it has been proved that if instead of the diagonally opposite corner squares being removed, one would remove *any* two squares of the opposite color, a solution is possible. I have never seen the proof.

23 - A statement that would work is: "You will not give me the penny." If the statement were false, then what it says is *not* the case, which means that I *would* give you the penny, but I can't give you either coin for a false statement, hence the statement must be true. Since it is true, then what it says *is* the case, I won't give you the penny. But I must give you one of the coins for a true statement, hence it must be the quarter.

This problem occurred to me in relation to Gödel's construction as follows: I thought of the quarter as the analogue of *truth* and the penny as the analogue of *provability,* and so the sentence "You will not give me the penny." is the analogue of the Gödel sentence, which effectively says "I am not provable."

24 - The only forbidden book is the Index.

25 -
  A: He's not a nice guy.
  B: *Yes,* he's not!
    or
  A: He's not a nice guy.
  B: *No,* he's not!

26 - First I will prove that Hypergame is normal: Well, the first move of Hypergame is to choose some normal game, and whichever one is chosen, it must terminate. Thus, Hypergame must terminate regardless of which normal game is chosen on the first move. This proves that Hypergame must be normal. But now, we have a problem: Since it is normal and in my first move I am allowed to choose *any* normal game, then I can say, "Let's play Hypergame." Then you can say, "Let's play Hypergame." Then I can say, "Let's play Hypergame," and so it is possible that the

Hypergame would never end, which proves that Hypergame is not normal after all. Thus, we have a true paradox. Hypergame cannot be considered either normal or not normal without contradiction!

27 - When I did this trick, what I said was "Either you will give me back one of the bills, or you will give me a billion dollars." Suppose the statement were false, then he would have to give me back one of the bills, as agreed, but that would make it *true* that he *either* gives me back one of the bills

Photo by Marilyn Smigiel.

or a billion dollars! Thus, the assumption that the statement is false leads to a contradiction, hence the statement must be true. Thus, he must either give me back one of the bills, or give me a billion dollars. But he can't give me back one of the bills, because the agreement was that if the sentence is true, then he must keep both bills! Thus, he owed me a billion dollars.

28 - What I wrote was, "You will write *no*. If he wrote *yes*, then he is claiming that the event would take place, which it didn't. If he wrote *no*, then he is claiming that the event will not take place, but in that case it did take place. Thus, whatever he writes is wrong!

29 - The fallacy was the assumption that each statement must be either true or false! Some statements can be neither true nor false without involving a contradiction. The statement on Envelope #2 was certainly false, since the bill was not in Envelope #1. But as to the sentence on Envelope #1, if it were true, we would have a logical contradiction, so it can't be true. It also can't be false, because the only way it could be false would be if the bill were in

Envelope #1, which it wasn't.

The whole purpose of this problem was to dramatically illustrate the principle discovered by the logician Alfred Tarski, that for languages like English, truth of sentences of the language is not definable within the language.

30 - What I said to her was: "You will give me neither your autograph nor a kiss." If the statement were true, she would have to give me her autograph, as agreed, but doing so would falsify the statement. Therefore, the statement can't be true; it must be false. Since it is false that she will give me *neither* one, she has to give me *either* one. But the agreement was that she wouldn't give me her autograph for a false statement; hence she had to give me a kiss!

31 - The answer is *zero*. The names were taken from the *phone book!*

32 - When I heard this problem, I said: "Well, the obvious answer is *the fourth rung from the bottom,* but it is too obvious to be right. I simply cannot see the error of my reasoning!" I was then told that the correct answer is *the* second rung from the bottom, because the boat rises with the water!

Bonus Problem - The answer is that this man had grandchildren who were really great! They were great grandchildren.

Colophon

Typeset in Helvetica Condensed Bold, Adobe's Caslon and Thinkers' Press' C.R. Horowitz.

Cover Design: Rob Long
Interior Art: Rob Long
Editing: Caren Laughlin, Bob Long, Raymond Smullyan, Nate Long

Special Thanks—Photos/Art/Articles

This biography is even more interesting because of the inclusion of properties from the following: Jack Gorn (early photos), Raymond and Blanche Smullyan (other photographs), Anatol Holt, Douglas Hofstadter, and Marvin and Gloria Minsky. Also, thanks to Leon Kirchner (photo), Robert Cowen (photo), Ann Close (photo), Martin Gardner (photo) and Peter Abramowitsch (photos). Drawings of the "Devil" and Frank Marshall taken with permission from *Lasker & His Contemporaries, vol. 3.*, art by Paul Herrera. Ed Marlo art by Paul Herrera from *The Sorcerer's Eyes*. Publicity still from Don Alan. Ray at the piano photo by Marilyn Smigiel. Ray at Amherst photo by Stacey Kennard; Alexander George. A.K. Peters for permission to reprint *Ambrose, Gardner and Doyle*.

Interior and exterior art produced by *LonGraphics*
P.O. Box 4401
Chatsworth, CA 91313-4401